Forthcoming titles

Vegetation Dynamics	John Miles
Sampling and Recording	R. Cormack

Further volumes are planned in the areas of modelling, population ecology, paleoecology and crop ecology.

Outline

Editors

George M. Dunnet
Regius Professor of Natural Histo
University of Aberdeen

Charles H. Gimingham
Professor of Botany,
University of Aberdeen

Editors' Foreword

Both in its theoretical and applied aspects, ecology is developing rapidly. In part because it offers a relatively new and fresh approach to biological enquiry, but it also stems from the revolution in public attitudes towards the quality of the human environment and the conservation of nature. There are today more professional ecologists than ever before, and the number of students seeking courses in ecology remains high. In schools as well as universities the teaching of ecology is now widely accepted as an essential component of biological education, but it is only within the past quarter of a century that this has come about. In the same period, the journals devoted to publication of ecological research have expanded in number and size, and books on aspects of ecology appear in ever-increasing numbers.

These are indications of a healthy and vigorous condition, which is satisfactory not only in regard to the progress of biological science but also because of the vital importance of ecological understanding to the well-being of man. However, such rapid advances bring their problems. The subject develops so rapidly in scope, depth and relevance that textbooks, or parts of them, soon become out-of-date or inappropriate for particular courses. The very width of the front across which the ecological approach is being applied to biological and environmental questions introduces difficulties: every teacher handles his subject in a different way and no two courses are identical in content.

This diversity, though stimulating and profitable, has the effect that no single text-book is likely to satisfy fully the needs of the student attending a course in ecology. Very often extracts from a wide range of books must be consulted, and while this may do no harm it is time-consuming and expensive. The present series has been designed to offer quite a large number of relatively small booklets, each on a restricted topic of fundamental importance which is likely to constitute a self-contained component of more comprehensive courses. A selection can then be made, at reasonable cost, of texts appropriate to particular courses or the interests of the reader. Each is written by an acknowledged expert in the subject, and is intended to offer an up-to-date, concise summary which will be of value to those engaged in teaching, research or applied ecology as well as to students.

Studies in Ecology

Island Ecology

M. L. GORMAN

Lecturer,
Department of Zoology,
University of Aberdeen

LONDON
CHAPMAN AND HALL
A Halsted Press Book, John Wiley & Sons, New York

First published in 1979
by Chapman and Hall Ltd
11 New Fetter Lane, London EC4P 4EE
© 1979 M. L. Gorman
Printed in Great Britain at the
University Press, Cambridge

ISBN 0 412 15540 0

Distributed in the USA
by Halsted Press, a Division of
John Wiley & Sons, Inc., New York

British Library Cataloging in Publication Data
Gorman, Martyn
    Island ecology – (Outline studies in ecology).
    1. Island ecology
    I. Title   II. Series
    574.5'0914'2   QH541.5.18   79-41166

    ISBN 0-412-15540-0

Contents

1 Introduction

The islands of the Pacific and East Indies made an enormous and fateful impact on the minds of Charles Darwin and Alfred Wallace, the fathers of modern evolutionary theory. Since then island floras and faunas have continued to play a central role in the development of evolutionary, and more recently ecological thought.

For much of this century island ecology was a descriptive science and a wealth of information has been amassed on patterns of species distributions, on the composition of island floras and faunas, on the classification of islands into types such as oceanic and continental, on the taxonomic description of insular species and sub-species and on the adaptations, often bizarre, of island creatures.

However, biologists are not satisfied for long with the mere collection of data and the description of patterns, but seek unifying theories. Island ecology was transformed into a predictive science by the publication, in 1967, of MacArthur and Wilson's *Theory of Island Biogeography*. This, perhaps the most influential book written on island ecology, has been the stimulus for a generation of theoretical ecologists and gifted field workers.

The books listed below in the bibliography will indicate to the reader the vast scope of island ecology and the changes in approach that have taken place over the years.

In the following chapters I discuss the work currently being carried out in the field of insular biogeography, some theoretical, some applied, some descriptive and some experimental. Not everyone will agree with the balance of material that I present but I hope that it will serve to whet the appetite of future island ecologists. Apart from anything else islands are marvellous places to be!

Bibliography

Wallace, A. R. (1880), *Island Life*, MacMillan, London.

Darlington, P. J. (1957), *Zoogeography. The geographical distribution of animals*, Wiley, New York.

Carlquist, S. (1965), *Island Life*, Natural History Press, New York.

MacArthur, R. H. & Wilson, E. O. (1967), *The Theory of Island Biogeography*, Princeton University Press, Princeton.

Cody, M. L. & Diamond, J. M. (Eds.) (1975), *Ecology and the Evolution of Communities*, Harvard University Press, Cambridge, Mass.

Lack, D. (1976), *Island Biology*, Blackwell Scientific Publications, Oxford.

2 Reaching and colonizing islands

2.1 Getting there

The easiest kinds of islands to reach have been those which were once part of a continent. Such land-bridge islands already had a fauna and flora when they became separated from the mainland.

Faced with the obvious difficulties that most organisms suffer in trying to cross salt water, biogeographers used to postulate that most remote islands were once linked to continents by land-bridges now sunk from view. Although this is true for some islands, we now know that many others have never been connected to mainlands in this way and that their biotas have of necessity arrived by dispersal across the open seas. There is a very large element of luck in any plant or animal arriving at an island in this way and the degree of luck needed increases with increasing remoteness. The palaeontologist G. G. Simpson used to talk of 'sweep-stake' dispersal, drawing an analogy with horse-race betting. Many people place money on the horses in a race, but few back the winner and very few back the outsider who wins at 100–1. In the same way many individuals get carried out to sea in one way or another, but very few reach and colonize an island and very few indeed reach the really remote islands such as the Hawaiian archipelago.

On these very remote islands the time intervals between successful colonizations can be amazingly long. In the Galapagos islands, recently dated by potassium-argon studies at some 3 million years old, the arrival of one plant species every 8000 years would be sufficient to account for the present, indigenous flora [19]. In the more remote Hawaiian group, where the major islands are about 5 million years old, the vascular plants need only have arrived at one species per 30 000 years, the land-snails one every 200 000 years and the birds one every 350 000 years. These intervals are awesome enough, but in reality are probably under-estimates since some of the smaller Hawaiian islands may be as old as 20 million years [1, 2, 24].

Although these figures underline the very real problems that organisms face in crossing the oceans of the world, the present distribution of plants and animals demands that it must take place. Indeed we have experimental and observational evidence to show that it can and does.

2.1.1 An experiment in sweep-stake dispersal

A unique, experimental study of dispersal has been made by Clark and McInerney [4]. The object of their study was a fresh-water fish, the Peamouth Chub (*Mylocheilus caurinus*), which lives in the rivers of

British Columbia and which is incapable of crossing more than a very few miles of salt-water. The Strait of Georgia, a 30 mile body of sea separating Vancouver Island from mainland Canada, therefore represents what should be an impassable barrier to the fish. And yet there are three confirmed records of the species on the island, those in the Nanaimo River and in Lake Somenos appearing to be natural invasions (Fig. 2.1). The estuary of the Nanaimo lies opposite the northern mouth of the mighty Fraser River and, while passage across the strait is highly improbable for most of the time, it can on occasions happen.

High salinity is the major problem facing a Peamouth Chub striving to reach Vancouver Island, but it is a problem which at times becomes less severe. The fresh water pouring out of the Fraser forms a corridor of low salinity surface water stretching out across the channel towards the island. The salinity gradient normally steepens sharply as one moves from the mouth of the Fraser but as the winter snows melt the river discharge increases and the wedge of low salinity water pushes further and further out into the strait. In some years the snow melt is very rapid and the discharge of the river so large that low salinities extend across the strait almost as far as Vancouver Island itself. 1951 was such a year; in June the surface salinity was below 15‰ right across the strait and below 13‰ for most of the way (Fig. 2.1).

Conditions such as these might allow the dispersal of the Chub across to Vancouver Island, but they occur only very infrequently; salinities of 12–15‰ at the western side of the strait have occurred on only 50 days in the last 30 years. Thus the route for colonization is restricted in both time and space: low salinity corridors occur only in years of rapid snow melt and these are of low probability.

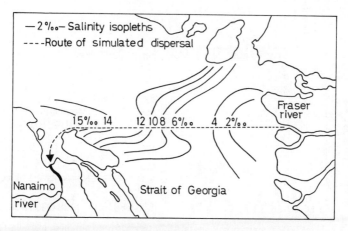

Fig. 2.1 Surface salinities in the Strait of Georgia, which separates British Columbia from Vancouver Island. The dotted line indicates a potential dispersal route from the Fraser River which was simulated in the laboratory and along which Peamouth Chub were forced to swim [4].

Given this set of environmental conditions which might permit dispersal, Clark and McInerney devised a simulated laboratory crossing of the Straits of Georgia in order to put it to the test. The simulated crossing was carried out in a performance tunnel in which a water pump provided a current against which a fish must swim if it was not to be swept back onto an electrified grid. The fish were caused to swim along a simulation of the transect shown in Fig. 2.1, each fish having to swim the appropriate distance and being exposed to the same salinity changes it would have encountered in a real crossing.

Ten fish were used in the simulated crossing and nine of them completed the 42 mile course, without difficulty, in 100 hours.

The value of this elegant experiment is that it shows that even highly improbable sea crossings can happen given the passage of sufficient time and the occurrence of the right conditions.

2.1.2 Dispersal observed

Only very rarely does the opportunity present itself to observe the colonization of an island *de novo*. Because of this, biogeographers interested in the process of dispersal usually have to resort to some kind of experimental study. One approach has been to observe the col-

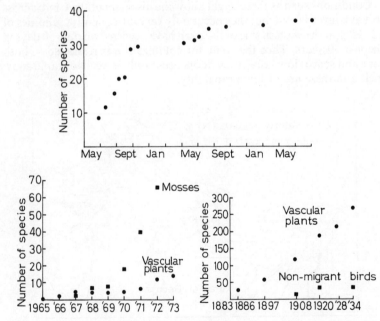

Fig. 2.2 Three real examples of colonization by dispersal from a distant source area. (*Top*) The number of insect species recorded from newly established nettle-beds over a period of three years [6]. (*Below left*) The number of species of mosses and vascular plants recorded on the new island of Surtsey from 1965–1973 [11]. (*Below right*) The recolonization of Krakatau by plants and birds [5, 10].

onization of new, man-made habitat islands such as the Dutch polders [7]. Simberloff and Wilson, in a series of imaginative experiments, fumigated whole mangrove islands in the Florida Keys in order to monitor the pattern of recolonization by arboreal arthropods [20, 23]. Others have created small habitat islands, for example bottles of sterile lake water, separated from a source area by inhospitable terrain [18]. In a recent study Davis planted plots of stinging nettles (*Urtica dioica*) 25 or 75 m from an old-established nettle-bed [6]. Within three years the plots had been colonized by 28 resident species of insects (Fig. 2.2).

Useful as such studies are, nature has provided the best experiments of

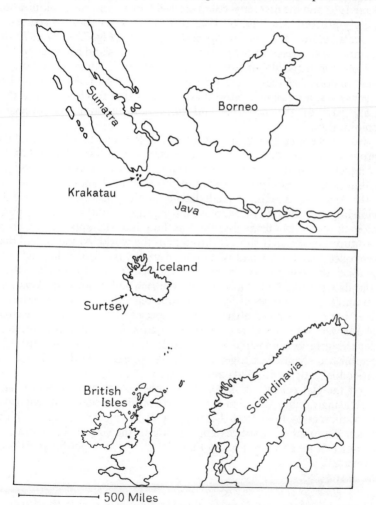

Fig. 2.3 Maps showing the position of the exploded island of Krakatau, now an Indonesian National Park, and the new volcanic island of Surtsey.

11

all. On November 14, 1963, the sea 40 km south-west of Iceland began to spew forth smoke and tephra in a volcanic eruption that was to last for three and a half years (Fig. 2.3). The following morning a new island called Surtsey, the island of the fire-giant Surtur, had risen clear of the waves. Although far out to sea it was not long before Surtsey began to receive living organisms, mainly from Iceland and the Westman islands. Just six months after the start of the eruption, bacteria, fungi, the fly *Dianesa zeryni*, various sea-birds and the seeds and vegetative parts of several beach plants, had all reached the new island [11]. The first established vascular plant, the sea-rocket *Cakile edentula*, was found in June 1965 and the first moss colony in 1967. From this start colonization slowly proceeded so that by 1973 there were 13 established species of vascular plants and over 66 species of mosses (Fig. 2.2). By 1970 the number of species of arthropods recorded on the island had risen to 158, which represents 20% of Iceland's total arthropod fauna. However, the vast majority of these were transient visitors who failed to establish themselves, a graphic illustration of the fact that reaching an island is only part of the problem and does not guarantee a successful colonization.

Surtsey lies in a hostile part of the world; the climate is severe and the growing season short. For these reasons colonization will not be complete for many years to come. In more equable parts of the world the colonization of volcanic islands can proceed much more rapidly.

In 1883, Krakatau, a small island in the East Indies (Fig. 2.3), violently exploded. In an eruption lasting three months, six cubic miles of rock was blown away and the ash flung into the upper atmosphere produced spectacular sunsets throughout the world. At the end all that remained was three small islets buried under 100 feet of hot ash and pumice and completely devoid of life. In contrast to Surtsey, these islands were rapidly colonized from the rich source areas of Java and Sumatra, only 15 miles away. After three years the ground was covered in a mat of blue-green algae while 11 species of ferns and 15 vascular plants were well established. Within 10 years the island was covered in dense vegetation and in the 50 years up to 1933, 271 species of plants had established themselves together with 36 species of birds, 5 lizards, a crocodile, a python, 3 bats and a rat (Fig. 2.2) [5, 10].

At the last census, in 1933, the number of plant species was still increasing rapidly although the number of bird species had reached a maximum as early as 1921. Clearly, highly mobile forms such as birds reach the number of species appropriate to the size of the island (see Chapter 3) much more rapidly than do groups with poorer powers of dispersal.

2.1.3 How do you get across an ocean?

The oceans of the world are clearly a formidable barrier to the dispersal of plants and animals, but they can be crossed. Plants, in particular, have evolved a fabulous variety of aids to assist in the dispersal of their seeds and much effort has been put into their description [2]. These adaptations have evolved primarily to allow relatively short movements within land masses, but given the opportunity they can carry plants far out to sea, to the remotest of islands. Some plants, particularly those living along the sea-shore, have seeds that can float in the sea unharmed for long periods of time. The seeds of the sea-rocket *Cakile edentula*, the first plant to colonize Surtsey were still 90% viable after 16 weeks in the sea [11]. Other species have sticky secretions, or mechanical hooks, on their seeds by which they become attached to the plumage of birds and in this way hitch a lift to distant parts. Many fruits contain seeds that are still viable after passing through an animals gut—most sewage farms have thriving tomato colonies! Such seeds may remain in a bird's body sufficiently long to be carried great distances. For example, snow buntings arriving on Surtsey after a journey from the British Isles had in their gizzards viable seeds of *Polygonom persicaria* and *Carex nigra* [11]. Even those seeds with no apparent special adaptations for dispersal may be picked up in mud by birds feet and carried off.

The wind is a powerful dispersal agent and many plants make use of it. The spores of ferns and mosses are so small ($< 100\ \mu$m) and light that they may be carried vast distances before returning to earth. Many seeds have structures which increase their wind resistance, for example the hairy tufts of the dandelion and other Compositae and the wings of rhodedendrons and sycamores.

As our knowledge of island floras has become more complete, botanists have been interested to determine the relative importance of these various methods of crossing the oceans. Obviously few plants will be seen actually arriving, but by examining the morphology of their seeds we can gain some insight into how it may have happened. Such examinations have been made for many island groups [2] and, as examples, analyses for the Hawaiian and Galapagos islands, and for the alpine floras of the African mountains, are shown in Table 2.1. The latter are habitat islands of boreal vegetation effectively separated from each other by seas of dry savanna.

Analyses of this kind indicate that the different methods of dispersal have been of varying importance in producing the floras of different

Table 2.1 The methods by which vascular plants have reached various islands.

Island group	% of the indigenous flora reaching the island by:					
	Ocean drift	Birds: sticky seeds	Birds: mud	Birds: internal	Birds: hooks etc.	Air flota- tion
Hawaii (2)	22.8	10.3	12.8	38.9	12.8	1.4
Galapagos (2)	23.1	8.5	13.7	27.7	22.8	4.3
Galapagos (19)	9	38.1	8.9	7.4	5	31
African Alps (12)	—	6.5	51	0	6.5	35

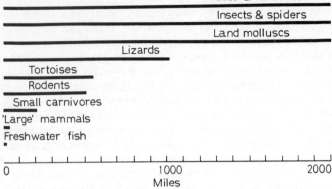

Fig. 2.4 The widest ocean gaps crossed by various groups of animals. These are extremes and are not necessarily typical of the whole group.

island groups, ocean drift being of paramount importance in this group, air flotation in that [2]. Attempts have been made to interpret these differences between floras in terms of an island's remoteness, its topography and climate and its prevailing winds and ocean currents. However, the fact that two workers can produce quite different analyses of the same flora, as shown for the Galapagos in Table 2.1, might suggest that such interpretations are premature.

Apart from those which can fly, animals can disperse to islands only by swimming or on the rafts of vegetation that are occasionally swept out to sea. For example, following the deluge of rain that fell on Fiji during the 1971 hurricane, rafts of vegetation up to thirty feet across were swept out of the Rewa river into the Pacific Ocean. From one such raft I collected three species of fresh-water molluscs and six arthropod species. The chances of such waifs making a landfall on a different island must be remote, but if such events happen during the passage of thousands of years some eventually will. The animals swept out to sea in this way will not be a random sample of those living on the mainland; those living along the sea shore, and in the estuaries of the rivers, will be greatly over-represented. Thus the beetle fauna living in the rotting vegetation on the strandline of the beaches of New South Wales is much more similar in composition to that of oceanic islands such as Samoa than it is to the fauna of the forest immediately behind the beaches [13].

Most land and fresh-water animals cannot survive in sea-water for long, but there are great differences in tolerance between taxa and some have managed to cross enormous water gaps either by swimming or on rafts (Fig. 2.4).

2.1.4 Super-tramps—dispersal as a way of life
Sometime in the early eighteenth century the island of Long, one of a

14

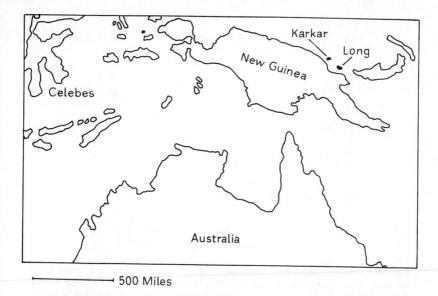

Fig. 2.5 The position of Long island, an island devastated by volcanic activity during the 18th century.

volcanic group lying between New Guinea and New Britain, exploded with the loss of all life (Fig. 2.5).

Today, some 200 years later, the ashy soils of lowland Long island are covered in an open savanna-like forest which supports fewer species of birds than does the lush rain forest of various neighbouring islands of similar size.

In 1972, Jared Diamond visited the island in the course of a survey of the avifauna of the islands of the Vitiaz and Dampier straits [8]. As he approached Long he was struck by the large numbers of birds leaving the island and flying out to sea. Clearly Long was producing numerous emigrants. Once on shore Diamond and his colleagues were immediately impressed by the spectacularly high densities at which the birds were living. Their subjective impressions were confirmed as soon as they started to catch birds in mist nets. The number of individual birds caught each day, per mist net, is a reasonable measure with which to compare relative population densities on different islands. On most of the islands in the area not devastated in recent time, the total population density of all bird species increased in a linear fashion with an increase in the number of species present (Fig. 2.6). On the island of Long, however, the population density was some five times higher than that on other islands, with similar numbers of species. Not all the 43 species living on Long were present in unusual numbers, rather the abnormally high density was due to huge populations of nine particular species. Diamond has termed these nine species super-tramps. They are species which have

15

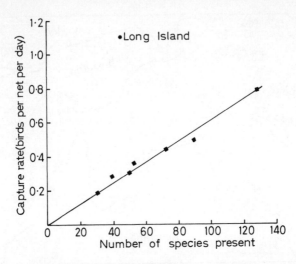

Fig. 2.6 The abundance of birds, measured by the rate at which they were caught in nets under standard conditions, on various islands between New Guinea and New Britain. Netting yields and therefore total population densities increase with the local number of species. On Long Island the population density is abnormally high [8].

been selected for their ability to disperse across open water and for their powers of rapid reproduction. These nine species are not resident on the large islands in the New Britain region; instead they specialize in occupying islands that are too small to maintain stable, long-lasting populations or islands devastated by volcanic eruption, tidal wave or hurricane. The price they pay for their powers of dispersal and reproduction is that they are eventually excluded from most islands by competitors that can exploit resources more efficiently and that can survive at lower resource abundances.

Whenever an island is denuded of its avifauna by some natural disaster the super-tramps, with their superior powers of dispersal, are first to arrive. They breed rapidly, often throughout the year, and soon fill the island. Further increases in population size produce surplus individuals who leave in search of new, empty islands, as Diamond has observed off Long. Eventually the island will be reached by other species, species with poor powers of dispersal but competively superior to the supertramp species. These later immigrants will eventually squeeze the supertramps out of existence on that island but by that time they will have ensured their survival as species by sending out emigrants in search of new pastures.

2.2 Establishing a beach-head

Getting to an island is only half the problem, even after arrival the chances of a successful colonization can still be very low. Perhaps the most hopeless situation will be where an individual of a sexually

16

reproducing species arrives alone, without a mate. Even when a pioneer population does become established from an asexual individual, a breeding pair or perhaps a pregnant female, it will be very vulnerable because of its small size and limited distribution. All populations are subject to random fluctuations, not only up, but also down and these can be disasterous for very small populations. Within a year of the formation of Surtsey the sea-rocket had established a beach-head colony of 20 seedlings and appeared set for a successful colonization. A very few weeks later, these hopes were dashed by a single, chance fall of ash from the crater Syrtlingur [11]. In order to grow past this vulnerable stage the colonizing population should have as large a rate of population increase as possible. The capacity for growth of some colonizing populations is quite remarkable as shown by the story of the mongoose *Herpestes auropunctatus*. By 1870 the sugar-cane plantations of Jamaica were losing at least £ 100 000 each year because of the ravages of rats. In an attempt to reduce the size of the offending rat populations a Mr. Espeut imported nine mongooses from Calcutta. Not to be outdone, estates on the other West Indian islands obtained individuals from Jamaica and by 1900 mongoose populations were firmly established on Cuba, Hispaniola, Puerto Rico, Trinidad, St. Croix, Buck, Vieques, St. Thomas, St. John, Tortola, St. Kit, Nevis, Antigua, Guadaloupe, Marie Galante, Martinique, St. Lucia, St. Vincent, Barbados, Grenada, and on the South American mainland in Surinam, British Guiana and French Guiana. Meanwhile, in 1883, seventy-two mongooses had been taken from Jamaica to the Hawaiian islands where populations were established on Maui, Molokai, Oahu and Hawaii. Also in 1883, a breeding pair was sent direct from India to Levuka in the Fiji islands where the species rapidly became established on Viti Levu and Vanua Levu, the two major islands of the group.

Thus within 30 years the descendants of just eleven animals had established populations throughout the Caribbean, on the continent of South America and on the island groups of Hawaii and Fiji.

There are species, however, which are quite unable to reach large population sizes on small islands, either because, like marshland birds, they have very special habitat requirements or because, as in the case of large carnivores or birds of prey, they need large feeding territories. Such species may never get beyond a vulnerable population size and will be generally absent from small islands. MacArthur and Wilson [17] have developed a model, based on *per capita* birth and death rates, in which a colonist is allowed to establish a population whose subsequent chance of extinction is treated as a random variable. The model predicts that the expected life of a population will be related to its size, populations numbered in tens or hundreds will become extinct fairly rapidly while those counted in thousands will persist indefinitely. In reality, the minimum size for a stable population will vary from species to species, but there is evidence that it is of importance in determining whether a species can survive on an isolated island. The first piece of evidence

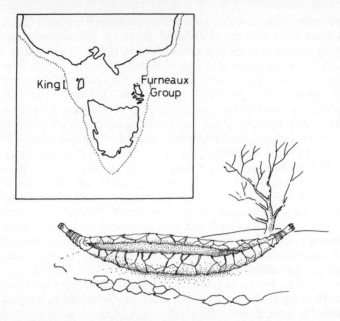

Fig. 2.7 The kind of bark canoe used by the peoples of Tasmania, King Island and the Furneaux group (from a contemporary print). The inset map shows by means of a dotted line the extent of dry land some 20 000 years ago.

comes from our own species (Fig. 2.7). Some 20–40 000 years ago, the sea-level was about 300 feet below its present level and what is now the island of Tasmania was connected to Australia by a bridge of dry land. Human beings walked across this bridge at least 22 000 years ago and settled the area [14]. When the seas rose again, at the end of the Pleistocene 12 000 years ago, most of the land-bridge was submerged and the humans were left stranded on the large island of Tasmania and, some 14 miles away, on King island (420 square miles) and the Furneaux group (770 square miles). Although within sight of Tasmania, the people living on King and Furneaux were completely cut off since their bark canoes rapidly became water logged in the sea and sank.

The Tasmanians survived long enough to be murdered by Europeans in the nineteenth century but the humans living on the King and Furneaux islands were extinct long before the arrival of the white man. Rhys Jones, the cultural anthropologist, has calculated that these latter islands could have supported only some 200–500 individuals and he reasons that isolated human populations of that order are far too small to survive for long [15].

A second example is provided by a recent study of island rodents [3]. The meadow vole (*Microtus pennsylvanicus*) is the only rodent present on a series of small islands lying off the coast of Maine, although the red-backed vole (*Clethrionomys gapperi*) is common on the adjacent

18

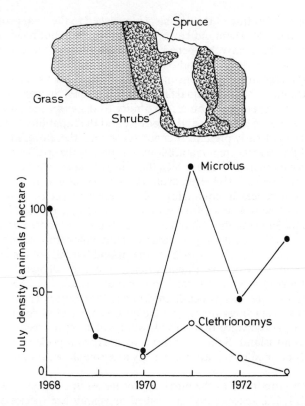

Fig. 2.8 A vegetation map for Rock Island. The graph shows the changes that took place in the density of vole populations following the introduction of 12 *Clethrionomys* individuals [3].

mainland. In the study, 12 individuals of *Clethrionomys* were introduced to Rock island (0.8 ha) where they rapidly displaced *Microtus* from the small area of woodland present. *Clethrionomys* was capable therefore of establishing itself on the island and of competing effectively with *Microtus*. However, as a species it has a rigid requirement for woodland and Rock island supports only a small plantation of spruce. The maximum size of the *Clethrionomys* population was thus severely limited, it never exceeded 30, and after three years of fluctuation it was extinct (Fig. 2.8). *Microtus* possesses a broader ecological flexibility and is capable of thriving in a variety of habitats. In this way it can maintain relatively high populations which survive on even small islands.

There is increasing evidence that island communities are not simply formed from the first species to arrive, they are not random combinations of the total species pool. Rather, colonists are selected, and co-adjusted in their niches and abundances, so as to fit together to form a stable, invasion-resistant species community in which the combined resource exploitation of the colonists is matched to the total production of the island [16]. Diamond has provided a detailed, but lucid, account of how this may have happened in the case of the avifauna of New Guinea and its satellite islands [9].

Clearly, reaching and colonizing an island is not an easy task, nor one that is accomplished with equal facility by all species. Success in this field requires very special attributes, an ability to disperse, the potential to increase in number rapidly and smoothly and the capability to integrate with species already present. It is not surprising, therefore, to find that successful colonists are not a random selection of the species present on the source mainland. We have seen that different taxa have very different powers of dispersal. However, even within a taxonomic group there are distinct differences in colonizing ability between species. Considering the birds of New Guinea for example, we find that of the 62 families there, only 36 reach the Solomons and 23 the Fiji islands. Sixteen New Guinea families contain particularly good colonizing species; they represent only 59% of the species of that island but 78% of the Solomon species and 84% of the Fijian species. We can recognize in these successful colonists certain common characteristics.

They tend to be social flock-living animals. Such species as white-eyes, thrushes and starlings are among the most successful of colonists since there is a good chance that a freak wind will carry a breeding pair or group to an island. Solitary species, such as woodpeckers, which are generally poor colonists, are more likely to arrive alone, without a sexual partner.

A high proportion of the birds, and other groups including ants and lizards [21, 22], successfully established on islands are species of freshwater, mangroves and secondary forest on the mainland. Such habitats have a scattered distribution and are often temporary in nature. This places a premium on mobility and the ability to breed rapidly when a new patch of habitat is found; they are in sense pre-adapted to island life.

Finally, colonizing species show considerable ecological flexibility, the ability to change aspects of their way of life such as their habitat or even their diet, depending upon the competitors they encounter on an island. We shall deal with this in more detail later but as an example we may note for now that the Island Thrush (*Turdus poliocephalus*) is confined to high mountain forest on New Guinea, but on Fiji it is common from the high mist forest right down to the coastal mangroves.

References

[1] Berger, A. J. (1972), *Hawaiian Bird-Life*, University of Hawaii Press, Honolulu.

[2] Carlquist, S. (1974), *Island Biology*, Columbia University Press, New York.

[3] Crowell, K. L. & Pimm, S. L. (1976), *Oikos*, **27**, 251–258.

[4] Clark, D. W. & McInerney, J. E. (1974), *Can. J. Zool.*, **52**, 457–469.

[5] Dammerman, K. W. (1948), *Verhandel.koninkl.Ned.Akad.Wetenschap.Afdel.Natuurk.*, **2** (44), 1–594.

[6] Davis, B. N. K. (1975), *J. Appl. Ecol.*, **12**, 1–14.

[7] der Boer, P. J. (1970), *Oecologia*, **4**, 1–28.

[8] Diamond, J. M. (1974), *Science*, **184**, 803–806.

[9] Diamond, J. M. (1975), *Ecology and Evolution of Communities* (ed. Cody M. L. and Diamond J. M.), pp. 342–443. Harvard University Press, Washington D.C.

[10] Docters van Leeuwen, W. M. (1936), *Ann. Jard. Botan. Buitenzorg*, **56–57**, 1–506.

[11] Fridriksson, S. (1975), *Surtsey, evolution of life on a volcanic island*, Butterworths, London.

[12] Hedborg, O. (1971), *Adaptive aspects of insular evolution* (ed. Stern), pp. 24–28, Washington State University Press.

[13] Howden, H. J. (1977), *Biotropica*, **9**, 53–57.

[14] Jones, R. (1973), *Nature*, **246**, 278.

[15] Jones, R. (1978), *Explorations in Ethno-Archaelogy* (ed. R. A. Gould), University of New Mexico Press, Albuquerque.

[16] MacArthur, R. H. (1972), *Geographical Ecology*, Harper and Row, New York.

[17] MacArthur, R. H. & Wilson, E. O. (1967), *The Theory of Island Biogeography*, Princeton University Press, Princeton.

[18] Maguire, B. (1963), *Ecol.Monogr.*, **33**, 161–185.

[19] Porter, D. M. (1976), *Nature*, **264**, 745–746.

[20] Simberloff, D. S. & Wilson, E. O. (1970), *Ecology*, **51**, 934–937.

[21] Williams, E. E. (1969), *Quart. Rev. Biol.*, **44**, 345–389.

[22] Wilson, E. O. (1961), *Am. Nat.* **95**, 169–193.

[23] Wilson, E. O. & Simberloff, D. S. (1969), *Ecology*, **50**, 267–278.

[24] Zimmerman, E. C. (1948), *Insects of Hawaii*, University of Hawaii Press, Honolulu.

3 How many species?

Great Britain has 44 species of indigenous terrestrial mammals, extant or recently extinct. In contrast Ireland, only 20 miles further into the Atlantic, has just 22. It could be argued that this simply reflects the difficulties that land mammals face in crossing water, were it not for the fact that it affects bats also; only 7 of Britain's 13 species breed in Ireland. Birds especially, have little difficulty in crossing water, indeed only 6 of Britain's 171 breeding species have not been recorded in Ireland, and yet 39 have never bred there and another 24 do so only occasionally. Why is there such a great difference in the numbers of species living and breeding on these two islands? Perhaps the most obvious difference between the two is that Great Britain is much larger than Ireland.

Throughout the world, larger islands support more species than smaller ones. Back in 1957, Darlington [3], on the basis of the numbers of reptiles and amphibians living on various West Indian islands, provided a neat rule of thumb; if one moves from one island to another only one tenth its size, the number of species of a particular taxonomic group will be halved. More generally, if the number of species in a given taxon is plotted against island area, both on log scales, a linear relationship results. Such a species-area curve is shown for the West Indian herpetofauna in Fig. 3.1.

This relationship between species number and island area is described by the simple equation

$$S = CA^Z$$

or, taking logs and rearranging, by the linear form

$$\log S = \log C + Z \log A$$

where S is the number of species in a given taxon, C is a constant giving the number of species when A has a value of 1, A is the area of the island and Z is the slope of the regression line relating S and A.

The value of C varies markedly from taxon to taxon and between different parts of the world, but Z is remarkably constant. A series of empirically derived values of Z for various real and habitat islands are shown in Table 3.1; most fall in the range 0.24–0.34.

The number of species increases with increased area of search on mainlands also. Consider for example, the number of species of flowering plants to be found in larger and larger sample areas of England (Fig. 3.1). In general, however, the value of Z for areas of

22

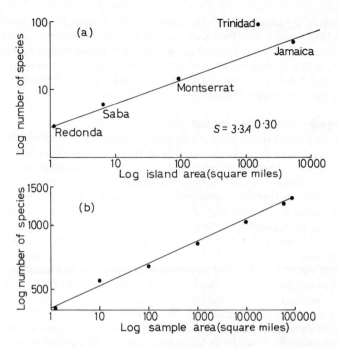

Fig. 3.1 (a) The number of Amphibian and Reptile species living on West Indian islands of various sizes. Note that Trinidad, joined to South America 10 000 years ago, lies well above the area-species curve of the other islands (after [11]).
(b) The area-species curve for the number of species of flowering plants found in sample areas of England [16].

mainland is much lower than that for islands and normally falls in the range 0.12–0.17. This means that small areas of mainland contain almost as many species as do large areas. The reason for this difference is that islands are isolated entities, with low levels of immigration, while continents are in a greater state of flux with organisms more easily moving from area to area. An important result is that an area of mainland will usually contain many more species than will a comparable island of the same size.

Why is there such a clear relationship between island area and

Table 3.1 Measured values of Z.

Taxonomic group	Island group	Z	Authority
Beetles	West Indies	0.34	[2]
Reptiles/amphibians	West Indies	0.30	[12]
Ants	Melanesia	0.30	[11]
Birds	East Indies	0.28	[7]
Diptera	Parks of Cincinatti	0.24	[6]
Land plants	Galapagos	0.33	[12]

23

richness of fauna and flora? The answer is neither simple nor generally agreed. At present two hypotheses, each with its proponents, dominate thought on the matter. The first argues that area in itself is not important except in that increased area will usually reflect increased topographical relief and habitat diversity. The second holds that differences in area alone may be responsible for differences in species numbers.

3.1 Species number and habitat diversity
It can be argued that since each habitat contains its own assemblage of plants and animals, a large island with more habitats should contain more species. Many ecologists have tried to measure the ecological diversity of islands and to correlate it statistically with species number. The problem is that the meaningful measurement of habitat diversity on a large scale is exceptionally difficult and there are, therefore, serious problems in measuring relative ecological differences among islands. The role of habitat diversity *per se* in determining the number of species present has rarely been defined. Instead, habitat differences are usually inferred via easily measured parameters that are believed to reflect such differences; island area, maximum elevation, the number of plant species present. Various workers have used the statistical technique of multiple regression to estimate the separate roles of these various parameters in determining the number of species of animals present on different islands. Thus in the Galapagos islands, 73% of the variation in the number of bird species living on different islands can be accounted for by differences in the number of plant species present [1, 8]. The forested mountain-tops of the American Great Basin form habitat islands in the sky separated by a sea of arid scrub. The numbers of boreal bird species on each mountain are not explained by differences in the area of woodland [9]. However, differences in an index of habitat diversity, based on the extent and complexity of coniferous forest, riparian woodland, wet meadow and aquatic habitat on each mountain account for some 91% of the variation in bird species number.

3.2 The effect of area alone
Despite empirical relationships between ecological diversity and the number of animal species there is evidence that large islands may contain more species than small ones, quite independently of differences in habitat diversity. For example, the parks of Cincinatti form habitat islands surrounded by an inhospitable sea of urban development. Differences in area alone account for 91% of the variation in the number of Diptera species living in different parks, while an index of habitat diversity makes no significant contribution [6].

The major problem is that for most islands, area and habitat diversity are inter-correlated and it is difficult to distinguish between their effects. Recently, an attempt has been made to separate the two variables by experimentally reducing the sizes of various islands while holding habitat diversity constant [13]. The experiment involved 8 small islands,

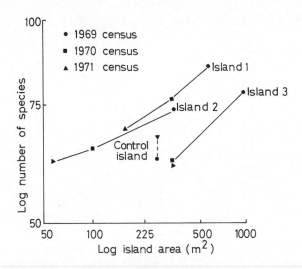

Fig. 3.2 The effect on the number of arthropod species of reducing the size of mangrove islands. Islands 1 and 2 were reduced after both the 1969 and the 1970 census. Island 3 was reduced once only after the 1969 census. The control island was not reduced, the change in species number being attributable to random fluctuation (after [13]).

in the Bay of Florida, each consisting of a pure stand of the mangrove *Rhizophora mangle*, and supporting various combinations of arboreal arthropods, insects, isopods, spiders and scorpions. After an initial faunal survey, teams of workers, armed with power-saws, physically removed parts of the islands, thus reducing their area. After a suitable delay the surveys were repeated. On four of the islands this was followed by a further reduction in island size and a third census. The outcome of the experiment was a clear demonstration that a reduction in island size leads to a reduction in species number despite there being no change in habitat diversity (Fig. 3.2). Why should this be so?

3.3 Equilibrium theory
More than a decade ago, MacArthur and Wilson [11] proposed a general statistical model of island biogeography which predicted, among other things, that larger islands would support more species than would smaller ones. The model represents the number of species on an island as a dynamic equilibrium resulting from a continuing immigration of new species to the island and the extinction of species already there. It implies that once equilibrium has been reached, the number of species present will remain relatively constant from year to year, although the composition of the species pool will change. The model is highly attractive; it is simple and yet it generates predictions which can be tested by field observations and experiments.

We can begin with a hypothetical island as yet having none of the species living on an adjacent mainland. MacArthur and Wilson

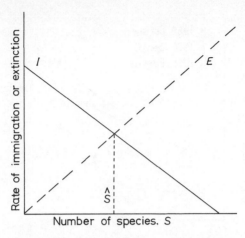

Fig. 3.3 A diagrammatic representation of an island's extinction curve E and immigration curve I, as functions of the number of species on the island, S. The equilibrium number of species for the island is $\hat{S}$, where the curves intersect.

reasoned that as species moved from the mainland to the island, the total immigration rate, the number of new species arriving per unit time, should decrease (Fig. 3.3). Initially, when there are few species on the island, the chance that an immigrant will belong to a new species will be high. Later as more and more species establish themselves on the island, the probability of an arrival being a new species will be much reduced. Hence the immigration rate of *new* species is a monotonic declining function of the number of species already present, S. The immigration rate would, of course, reach zero when all the species present on the mainland had colonized the island.

However, this is unlikely to happen. As the number of species on the island increases, the rate of extinction of the species present will increase (Fig. 3.3). This is because on the one hand there are now simply more species available to become extinct, but also because when more species are present, each will be rarer due to competition and will be more prone to random extinction. At the point where the immigration and extinction curves cross, immigration and extinction rates are equal, new species are arriving at the same rate as old ones are becoming extinct (Fig. 3.3). The number of species on the island has now reached an equilibrium $\hat{S}$, but an equilibrium which is dynamic and which results from a continuing turnover of species.

The basis of the model is therefore to plot I, the number of species arriving per unit time and E, the number becoming extinct, against S, the number of species on the island at any one time. As a simple approximation we may assume that I and E are linear functions of S. Do you think that this is a reasonable assumption?

So far we have dealt with total immigration and extinction rates. The average immigration rate of new species, per species available for colonization when S species are already present, is given by

$$\lambda = \frac{I}{P - S} \text{ or } I = \lambda(P - S) \tag{1}$$

where P is the number of species on the mainland, and $P - S$ the number not yet on the island.

The average extinction rate of species, per species on the island is

$$\mu = \frac{E}{S} \tag{2}$$

The rate at which species on the island increase with time (dS/dt) is given by

$$\frac{dS}{dt} = I - E \text{ or } \frac{dS}{dt} = \lambda(P - S) - \mu S \tag{3}$$

At equilibrium dS/dt is zero by definition and since at this point $S = \hat{S}$

$$\lambda(P - \hat{S}) - \mu\hat{S} = 0 \tag{4}$$

or by rearrangement

$$\hat{S} = \frac{\lambda P}{\lambda + \mu} \tag{5}$$

Thus given a knowledge of immigration and extinction rates, and these are very hard to measure, we can predict the number of species at equilibrium. These very basic equations can be put to further use, to make other predictions. For example by solving the differential Equation 3, it is possible to calculate S at any point in time

$$S = \frac{\lambda P}{\lambda + \mu}(1 - e^{-(\lambda + \mu)t}) \tag{6}$$

where e is the base of natural logarithms. As t in Equation 6 gets larger and larger, the expression

$$e^{-(\lambda + \mu)t}$$

approaches zero and, of course, S approaches $\hat{S}$, with the result that eventually $\hat{S} = \lambda P/\lambda + \mu$, as in Equation 5.

MacArthur and Wilson use this gradual climb to equilibrium (some islands decline to equilibrium as we shall see in Chapter 7) to derive an equation giving the rate of turnover, which equals the immigration or extinction rate, at equilibrium.

First they select an arbitrary fraction, 90%, of $\hat{S}$, or $0.9\hat{S}$. Substituting this into Equation 5 we find

$$0.9\hat{S} = \frac{\lambda P}{\lambda + \mu} \times 0.9 \tag{7}$$

27

or by using Equation 6 we obtain

$$S = 0.9\hat{S} = \frac{\lambda P}{\lambda + \mu}(1 - e^{-(\lambda + \mu)t_{0.9}}) \tag{8}$$

If we inspect Equations 7 and 8 carefully it is apparent that

$$1 - e^{-(\lambda + \mu)t_{0.9}} = 0.9 \tag{9}$$

where $t_{0.9}$ is the time required for an island to fill to 90% of its equilibrium number of species. If we rearrange Equation 9 and take natural logs

$$t_{0.9} = \frac{2.3}{\lambda + \mu} \tag{10}$$

3.3.1 The effects of size and remoteness

We can now consider what factors influence the number of species at equilibrium. The model allows us to make several predictions. Imagine two islands of similar size and topography but at different distances to

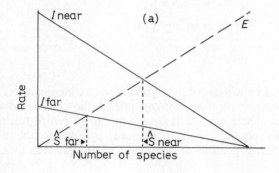

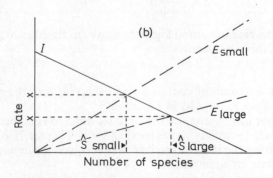

Fig. 3.4 (a) Immigration rates decrease with increasing distance from source areas. Distant islands therefore have fewer species at equilibrium than do near ones.
(b) Extinction rates should vary inversely with island size. Consequently small islands will reach equilibrium with a lower number of species than will larger ones. Note also that the small island will have a higher rate of turnover of species X than will a larger one.

the source mainland. Clearly organisms will reach the near island with relative ease but the far one only with difficulty. The immigration rate to the near island will therefore be greater than that to the far island (Fig. 3.4). Since the rate of extinction is unlikely to be affected by distance it will be similar for both islands, with the result that the near island will hold more species at equilibrium (Fig. 3.4). Because of their lower immigration rates, distant islands will take longer to reach equilibrium, indeed many ancient but remote islands, such as the Hawaiis, probably have yet to reach equilibrium.

We may also consider the influence of island area: imagine now two islands at the same distance from the mainland but one much larger than the other. Since they are equally accessible they will enjoy similar immigration rates (Fig. 3.4). However, the smaller island will usually support smaller populations of any species than will the larger one. It can be shown statistically [11], that while every finite population will become extinct eventually, small equilibrial populations numbered in tens or hundreds will do so rapidly while large ones numbered in hundreds of thousands will last almost indefinitely. The immediate cause of extinction for small populations may be chance catastrophe or even random variation in population size (see Chapter 2). We might expect, therefore, that the smaller island would have a higher rate of extinction and that it would hold fewer species at equilibrium (Fig. 3.4). Furthermore, if the model is correct, the smaller island would be expected to have a higher rate of turnover of species at equilibrium, X, than would the large one.

So much for the model itself; do we have empirical evidence that it describes accurately what happens in the real world? We might consider four of the predictions made by the model, in relation to field observations and experiments.

(1) The number of species on an island should remain constant with time.
(2) Despite this constancy of number, over a period of time species should become extinct.
(3) Equally, extinctions should be balanced by immigrations.
(4) The rate of turnover of species should vary inversely with island area.

Support for these predictions comes from a variety of studies. The species of birds breeding on the Channel Islands off California have been censused on a number of occasions since the end of the last century [10]. The numbers of species on most of the islands have remained remarkably constant, as predicted by the model (Fig. 3.5).

Despite such constancy of number, the various censuses reveal that species do become extinct, to be replaced by new immigrants. In the case of the Californian Channel Islands, censuses carried out 50 years apart reveal that 0.3–1.2% of the breeding species are annually replaced by new species on large and small islands respectively (Fig. 3.6). These rates

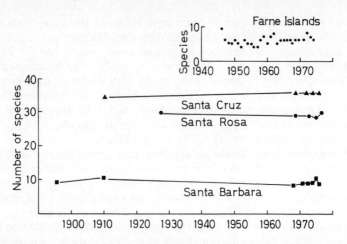

Fig. 3.5 Fluctuations in the number of species of birds breeding on various Californian Channel islands and on the British Farne islands. Note the high degree of stability in species number [5,10].

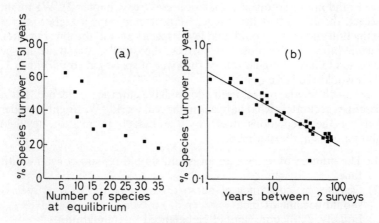

Fig. 3.6 (a) Species turnover on nine Californian Channel islands. the ordinate gives the percentage of the species pool replaced by new species over a period of 51 years. The abscissa is the number of species on each of the islands. Note that the largest islands, those with the most species, have the lowest rates of turnover [4].
(b) Turnover rates on the Californian Channel island Anacapa, as a function of the time elapsed between the two surveys. The turnover rate apparently decreases with increased time between surveys due to undetected colonizations and extinctions [10].

are probably underestimates of turnover since with an inter-census interval of 50 years, many species could become established and subsequently extinct unnoticed. Recent, annual censuses show that long interval studies underestimate turnover rates by a factor of 10 due to undetected in-and-out movements by species [5]. For example, annual

30

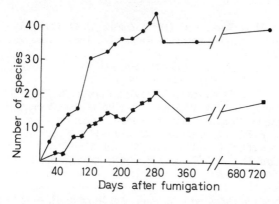

Fig. 3.7 The pattern of colonization, by arthropods, of two mangrove islands following complete fumigation. The number of species rose rapidly with time but soon levelled off at numbers comparable to those before fumigation [15].

surveys show that the island of Anacapa has a turnover rate of 3.7%/year while two surveys 67 years apart indicate a value of only 0.41%/year (Fig. 3.6). Thus turnover rates among the Channel Islands are probably of the order 0.5–1.4%/year for large islands and 0.8–4.9%/year for small ones. Such species turnover, and its inverse relationship to island area is exactly as predicted by equilibrium theory.

Further support comes from a very different, but elegant, experimental study of mangrove islands among the Florida Keys [14, 15]. Simberloff and Wilson counted all the species of arboreal arthropods living on a series of small islands. They then handed over to professional pest-controllers who erected scaffolding and covered the islands with enormous plastic bags before pumping in methyl bromide, thus killing the arthropods. Then, by repeated census, they followed the process of colonization over the next two years. The fumigated islands were rapidly recolonized and within 200 days, an equilibrium had been reached that was essentially the same as that measured prior to fumigation (Fig. 3.7). However, at the end of this time, the species composition of the fauna was quite different from what it had been before fumigation. For example one island supported 7 species of Hymenoptera prior to fumigation, and had 8 some 360 days after. Only 2 of these species were present on both occasions however.

All of these findings, observational and experimental, are as predicted by the equilibrium model, and provide powerful support for its validity.

References

[1] Abbot, I., Abbot, L. K. & Grant, P. R. (1977), *Ecol. Monogr.*, **47**, 151–184.
[2] Darlington, P. J. (1943), *Ecol. Monogr.*, **13**, 37–61
[3] Darlington, P. J. (1957), *Zoogeography*, Wiley, New York.
[4] Diamond, J. M. (1969), *Proc. Nat. Acad. Sci.*, **64**, 57–63.
[5] Diamond, J. M. & May, R. (1978), *Science*, **197**, 266–270.

[6] Faeth, S. H. & Kane, T. C. (1978), *Oecologia*, **32**, 127–133.

[7] Hamilton, T. H., Barth, R. H. & Rubinoff, I. (1964), *Proc. Nat. Acad. Sci.*, **52**, 132–140.

[8] Harris, M. P. (1973), *Condor*, **75**, 265–278.

[9] Johnson, N. K. (1975), *Evolution*, **29**, 545–567.

[10] Jones, H. L. & Diamond, J. M. (1976), *Condor*, **78**, 526–549.

[11] MacArthur, R. H. & Wilson, E. O. (1967), *The Theory of Island Biogeography*, Princeton University Press, Princeton.

[12] Preston, F. W. (1962), *Ecology*, **43**, 410–432.

[13] Simberloff, D. S. (1976), *Ecology*, **57**, 629–648.

[14] Simberloff, D. S. & Wilson, E. O. (1969), *Ecology*, **50**, 278–296.

[15] Simberloff, D. S. & Wilson, E. O. (1970), *Ecology*, **51**, 934–937.

[16] Williams, C. B. (1964), *Patterns in the Balance of Nature and Related Problems in Quantitative Ecology*, Academic Press, New York.

4 Islands as experiments in competition

One of the central problems of ecology is that of the role played by competition in determining the species composition of a community. There is an extensive literature on the experimental and theoretical nature of competition [e.g. 1, 10, 11] but here we may be satisfied with MacArthur's simple definition: two species are competitors if an increase in either harms the other.

In the real world, competition is very difficult to study; it is subtle and need not happen very often to be important. Very rarely do we see overt competition, animals fighting over the same scrap of food or nest-site. However, many ecologists become convinced of its importance from the indirect evidence of differences in species distribution patterns and feeding requirements. It seems likely that if species are to co-exist then they must avoid continuing, direct competition, which is to say that they must have different ecological requirements. (*How* different co-existing species must be is an important but unanswered question). Such ecological separation, or sorting of species, could be achieved in a number of ways. Congeners could be spatially separated from each other by virtue of occupying different geographical areas, different habitats in the same area or different vertical strata in the vegetation of the same habitat. Alternatively they could co-exist but avoid direct competition by exploiting different food supplies or the same food in different ways.

When we come to look at the species living on mainlands, particularly in the species-rich tropics, we find that they are indeed often restricted to narrow altitudinal ranges, to single habitats and to narrow vertical strata in the vegetation. Thus Terborgh, working in the mountains of Peru, has found that the altitudinal ranges of closely related species abut each other, or leave gaps, but do not overlap [15]. Diamond [3] has made similar discoveries in the mountains of New Guinea and its neighbouring islands (Fig. 4.1). The most simple explanation of such observations is that species are restricted to narrow altitudinal bands not by intrinsic adaptations but by competition with neighbouring congeners.

In Africa, at Usambara, 400 species of birds breed in lowland and montane rainforest, in grassland and in savanna. Moreau [12] reports that not a single species breeds in more than one of these habitats, indeed considering just the lowland rainforest, only 2% of species occupy both the interior and the edge. Again the most simple explanation is that species are restricted to particular habitats by competition with species of similar ecological requirements.

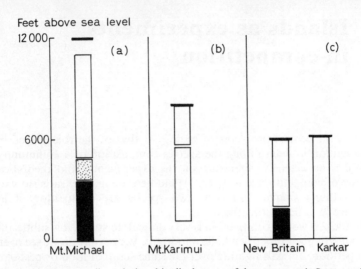

Fig. 4.1 (a) The mutually exclusive altitudinal ranges of three congeneric flower-peckers on a New Guinea mountain. The summit is shown by the horizontal line. The top species is *Melanocharis nigra*, the middle one *M. longicauda* and the bottom one *M. versteri*.
(b) Altitudinal distributions of the warblers *Crateroscelis robusta* and *C. murina* on Mt. Karimui. Note that the two species replace each other sharply at 5400 feet.
(c) Altitudinal ranges of 2 congeneric lorikeets on mountains in New Britain and Karkar island. *Charmosyna placentis* (solid bar) and *C. rubrigularis* (open bar) have exclusive ranges on Mt. Talawe. Only *C. rubrigularis* has colonized Karkar and there it expands into the range of its absent congener [2].

In many island archipelagoes closely related species of apparently similar ecology have mutually exclusive geographical ranges. Such distributions are frequently cited as one of the strongest pieces of evidence for interspecific competition. For example, in the Fiji islands four dove species, *Ptilinopus porphyraceus, P. victor, P. luteovirens* and *P. layardi* have exclusive ranges with no two species being found on the same island (Fig. 4.2). The distances between the islands are relatively small and it seems unlikely that the doves are unable to fly from one island to another.

However, the unconvinced could argue that exclusive geographical ranges simply reflect the chance failure of species to invade the islands from which they are absent. Stronger evidence comes from dynamic systems where a species is seen to expand its range into that of a putative competitor and to replace it rather than to co-exist. The ant *Pheidole megacephala* was originally found only in central Africa but during a phase of expansion reached the island of Madeira where it virtually eliminated the native ant fauna. Years later *Iridomyrmex humilis* reached Madeira from South America and by the late 1890s had, in its turn, completely replaced *P. megacephala* [2, 7].

Such observations, fascinating as they are, are at best only indirect

34

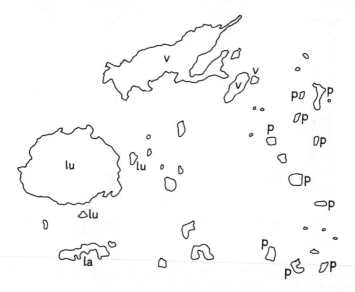

Fig. 4.2 The mutually exclusive ranges of *Ptilinopus* doves in Fiji. v. *Ptilinopus victor*; lu, *P. luteovirens*; la, *P. layardi*; p, *P. porphyraceus*. Note that no island has two species.

evidence of competition. Ideally one would wish to carry out experiments on the grand scale in which certain species could be removed and the response of the remaining species monitored. If species are indeed restricted to different areas, habitats, altitudinal belts or vegetational strata by competition, then removal of competitors should result in an expansion of the use made of these parameters by the remaining species.

Clearly, such manipulations would be rather difficult to arrange, but happily islands provide ready-made, natural experiments. We have seen already that islands have fewer species than do mainland areas of similar size, latitude and topographical relief. It follows that insular species will be co-existing with fewer competitors than will their mainland counterparts. Islands offer an opportunity, therefore, of investigating to what extent the abundance and observed niche of a species is determined by its genetic nature, and to what extent by competition. Since competition should restrict the abundance of a species and its utilization of resources, one would predict that island populations would live at higher densities and would have broader niches than their mainland relatives. Recent comparisons of island and mainland populations have shown that insular species do exhibit a variety of ecological differences in support of such a prediction. These responses, which have been termed 'ecological release' or 'niche expansion', include increased population density, the utilization of a wider range of habitats and altitudes and changes in diet and foraging behaviour.

These changes, which may be evolutionary or short-term behavioural

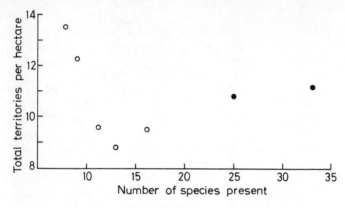

Fig. 4.3 Bird densities, measured as the number of territories per hectare, on several Swedish islands (open circles) and plots of the mainland (closed circles) supporting different numbers of species [13].

adaptations, form some of the best evidence for the importance of competition in structuring vertebrate communities.

4.1. Abundance shifts
Nilsson [13] has examined the breeding birds on 39 small islands and in two mainland areas at Lake Mockeln, Sweden. He finds that the combined densities of birds are similar on the mainland and on the islands, despite there being far fewer species on the islands (Fig. 4.3). It is hard to avoid the conclusion that competition limits the abundance of individual species on the mainland.

Again, on Puercos in the Pearl archipelago, there are less than half as many species as there are on similar areas of the Panama mainland [11]. The abundance per species is much higher on the island however, 1.35 pairs/species/hectare as compared to 0.28 on Panama.

4.2 Altitudinal shifts
We have seen that, on mainlands, related species avoid competition by occupying mutually exclusive altitudinal zones. This is extremely rare on islands: for example, on Viti Levu in the Fijis the majority of bird species are to be found from sea-level to the tops of the mountains. On New Guinea, the Island Thrush *Turdus poliocephalus* is confined to altitudes above 2750 m, lower altitudes being divided among several congeneric competitors; while on Fiji, where these competitors are absent, *T. poliocephalus* is found from the highest elevations right down to sea-level [6].

On New Britain the two congeneric Lories *Charmosyna placentis* and *C. rubrigularis* enjoy mutually exclusive altitudinal distributions, but on Karkar island only *C. rubrigularis* is present and here it expands down to sea-level occupying the altitudes normally taken by its absent congener [Fig. 4.1].

36

4.3. Habitat shifts

On New Guinea, five congeneric species of the Kingfisher *Halcyon* segregate on the basis of habitat. Only one of these species, *Halcyon chloris*, has colonized Fiji. Restricted in New Guinea to coastal mangrove forests, in Fiji it occupies all major habitats from mangroves to montane rainforest and dry grasslands [6]. Diamond and Marshall [5] give many other examples of habitat shifts among the New Hebridean avifauna.

4.4. Shifts in vertical foraging range

The pigeon *Columba vitiensis* feeds only in the canopies on New Guinea, while its congener *C. pallidiceps* feeds on the ground. Only *C. vitienesis* has reached Fiji and there it feeds not only in the trees but also on the ground in the manner of its absent relative.

   Lister [9], in a study of West Indian lizards, has shown that the height at which *Anolis sagrei* feeds in the forest is a function of how many congeners are present. On Jamaica, where it faces six congeneric competitors, it has a very narrow range of perch heights, while on islands such as Albaco and Cayman Brac where it is the only anolid present it feeds over a wide vertical range (Fig. 4.4). One concludes that on Jamaica its vertical distribution is limited by competition with related species and that in their absence it expands its foraging range.

4.5. Dietary shifts

The most surprising shifts, and ones which may involve more than

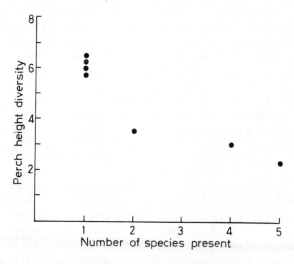

Fig. 4.4 The diversity of perch heights utilized by female *Anolis sagrei* on various West Indian islands plotted against the number of competing species they face. There is a clear tendency for *A. sagrei* to occupy a broader set of perch heights as the number of competitors decreases [6].

behavioural plasticity, are changes in diet. Consequently they are among the rarest niche changes we know of.

On New Guinea the role of seed-eater in open grassland is filled by various *Lonchura* finches while the parrot-finches *Erythrura* make a living eating figs and buds in the forest.

The *Lonchura* finches have failed to reach Fiji and the open grasslands of the islands are exploited by *Erythrura pealii*. *Erythrura kleinschmidti* lives in the rainforest, eating figs as it should, but also acting like a honey eater by snipping off the bases of flowers and drinking nectar! Such major shifts are of great interest; a major problem awaiting attack is that of the relative roles of behavioural and genetic changes.

4.6. Assembly rules for island communities

Competition is difficult to study even when only a pair of species is involved. In the real world, however, only rarely is one dealing with such simple situations. More usually, one is concerned with a whole community of organisms in which each species is competitively impinged upon, to differing degrees, by a whole range of other species. MacArthur [11] has termed interactions of this order diffuse competition. Indirect evidence for its existance can again be obtained from a perusal of the distribution of organisms. For example, the Bananaquit *Coereba flaveola* is an extremely abundant bird on all the islands of the West Indies, except for Cuba from which it is absent.

There is no single competitor on Cuba which might exclude the Bananaquit and one is forced to the conclusion that the Cuban avifauna exploits resources so thoroughly that the Bananaquit has been unable to establish a beach-head. In a similar manner, among the Fiji islands the Silktail *Lamprolia victoriae* is found only on Vanua Levu and Taveuni. Again the other islands have no single species which might possibly exclude it, indeed they have no species in the same family!

Recent studies contend that this kind of diffuse competition is a major factor in determining the composition of island faunas. For example, Diamond [4] argues that avifaunas are not chance assemblages of species but that colonization is essentially a deterministic process. Through diffuse competition, he argues, the component species of a community are selected and co-adjusted in their niches so as to fit together and to exploit the available resources so thoroughly that further invasions by new species are very difficult.

Using the faunal lists from 50 satellite islands of New Guinea, Diamond has made an attempt to derive assembly rules for them; statements of the different avian communities that could possibly exist on a particular island of given size. His conclusions are that the permitted combinations are relatively few. He starts his analysis by constructing incidence functions for each species and finds that species fall into three broad categories depending upon the types of islands on which they are found. The first category of species are found only on species-rich islands. The second, called tramps, are also found on species-rich islands but also, with a lower probability, on species-poor islands. The third group, the supertramps, are confined to the species-poor islands. Is this all the information we need if we are to predict how communities might be assembled from the total species pool? Apparently not; one needs to invoke two rules as well.

The first, compatability rules, are based on the observed mutually exclusive ranges of pairs of species and state that certain closely related species cannot, under any circumstances, co-exist. Combination rules are similar in basis to compatability rules but are based on diffuse competition which prevents certain combinations of groups of species from co-existing. Combination rules are derived from incidence functions by calculating the 'expected' probability of a given combination of species being found together on an island of given size. This is done by multiplying together the individual probabilities of individual species being found on such an island. The outcome is that certain combinations are found less often than expected, or not at all.

Such incidence functions, compatability rules and combination rules are finally married to form assembly rules. These analyses, although they hold great promise, are at an early stage. The analysis of the New Guinea satellite islands is in some ways unsatisfactory. With only 50 islands, the number in each size category is small and the absence of a particular combination may not indicate an underlying incompatability of species, but may merely be due to chance. More seriously, the rules formulated by Diamond lack predictive power in that all the data were required before the rules could be formulated and predictions made.

Diamond's analysis suggests a highly deterministic form of island colonization in which the only stochastic element is the order in which the first colonists arrive. On this depends which of the few possible communities will be the outcome.

Although vertebrate data are usually interpreted in the light of such competitive interactions, botanists and invertebrate zoologists often seek to explain distributions simply in terms of the responses of individual species to the environmental hazards they face. Many such workers would argue that colonization is essentially a stochastic process, akin to shooting arrows each of which have similar chances of hitting the butt, and that in the absence of competition the distribution of island organisms would be much as they are today.

Whether this is true or not must wait on more detailed statistical analyses of community structures. But until then we must follow Simberloff's [14] advice and not discard Occam's razor in seeking different explanations for the distributions of different taxa.

References
[1] Cody, M. L. & Diamond, J. M. (eds.) (1975), *Ecology and the evolution of communities*, Harvard University Press, Cambridge, Mass.
[2] Crowell, K. L. (1968), *Ecology*, **49**, 551–555.
[3] Diamond, J. M. (1970), *Proc. Nat. Acad. Sci.*, **67**, 529–536.

[4] Diamond, J. M. (1975), Assembly of species communities. In *Ecology and The evolution of communities* (ed. Cody, M. L. & Diamond, J. M.), Harvard University Press, Cambridge, Mass.

[5] Diamond, J. M. & Marshall, A. G. (1977), *Emu*, **77**, 61–72.

[6] Gorman, M. L. (1975), *Ibis*, **117**, 152–161.

[7] Haskins, C. P. & Haskins, E. F. (1965), *Ecology*, **46**, 736–740.

[8] Karr, J. R. (1971), *Ecol. Monogr.*, **41**, 207–233.

[9] Lister, B. C. (1976), *Evolution*, **30**, 659–676.

[10] May, R. M. (ed.) (1976), *Theoretical Ecology*, Blackwell, Oxford.

[11] MacArthur, R. H. (1972), *Geographical Ecology*, Harper & Row, New York.

[12] Moreau, R. E. (1948), *J. Anim. Ecol.*, **17**, 113–126.

[13] Nilsson, S. G. (1977), *Oikos*, **28**, 170–176.

[14] Simberloff, D. S. (1978), *Am. Nat.*, **112**, 713–726.

[15] Terborgh, J. (1971), *Ecology*, **52**, 23–40.

5 The very remote islands

Only a limited number of species can co-exist successfully on an island. The available niches are filled, as we have seen in Chapter 3, by a continuous turnover of species derived from an adjoining mainland or from some other island.

There are circumstances, however, in which niches are filled not by immigrant species but by species generated within an island, or island archipelago. Speciation takes place when populations originally derived from a single ancestral species acquire reproductive isolation from each other and become so different in their ecological requirements that sympatric existence becomes possible. This usually demands that populations are geographically separated by some physical barrier, open water or perhaps a mountain range, so that gene flow between them is greatly reduced.

When speciation proceeds so far as to produce a series of closely related species, with different ecological requirements, we term it adaptive radiation. For the niches of an island to be filled by adaptive radiation, rather than by the immigration of species from elsewhere, two factors must be satisfied.

Firstly, if speciation is to occur within the confines of a single island, then the island must be large enough and with sufficient topographical relief for the effective isolation of populations. The minimum area required will vary markedly from taxon to taxon. Among the Pacific islands, for example, speciation of birds has taken place only on New Guinea, Australia and possibly New Zealand, while many other taxa, such as the insects, lizards and angiosperms, have speciated on New Caledonia and even smaller islands [2]. The important difference between these taxa is that of their powers of dispersal. An island which appears small to a highly mobile animal such as a bird, may be effectively very large for an angiosperm with limited dispersal ability. On the other Pacific islands, bird speciation has been possible only across the water gaps separating the islands of an archipelago or the gaps between archipelagos themselves [3].

Above all else, adaptive radiation is a product of difficulty of dispersal to an island, whether the difficulty be due to distance or to adverse winds and currents. The likelihood of speciation occurring within an archipelago increases with distance from the source area and reaches a maximum on archipelagos at the very limit of the dispersal powers of the taxon concerned. This is because on very remote islands, or archipelagos, colonists will arrive only very rarely and will not, therefore, fill the available niches before speciation from within can occur. Different groups of plants and animals possess very different dispersal abilities and consequently adaptive radiation can take place on islands at very different distances from the source area; conifers have radiated on New Caledonia, ants in Fiji, frogs in the Seychelles, but ferns and birds only on very remote islands such as the Hawaiian group.

The spectacular ability for dispersal which allows a species to reach and spread through a remote archipelago must subsequently be lost; only in this way can gene flow between island populations be reduced so as to allow the achievement of reproductive isolation and ecological segregation. This tendency for island populations to lose their powers of dispersal is well known, Carlquist (2) describes in graphic detail the many cases of seeds losing their parachutes, insects their wings, and birds, such as the dodo and moas, their ability or inclination to fly. To give a specific example, the ancestors of the musk-parrot *Prosopeia* flew thousands of miles to reach the Fiji islands and yet the species living on Gau is never seen on Viti Levu, only 25 miles away. They fly perfectly well but like so many island species and races they have a psychological barrier to crossing water gaps.

Let us now take a look at two very different examples of adaptive radiation; one has taken place on a single island and the other within an archipelago.

Fig. 5.1 Morphological variation among the ancient conifers of New Caledonia (Top left) *Araucaria cooki*. (Top right) *A. rulei*. (Below left) *A. montana*. (Middle) *A. bernieri*. (Bottom right) *A. muelleri*.

5.1 The ancient conifers of New Caledonia

The conifers are a truly ancient group; first seen in the Carboniferous 200 million years ago, they have seen the rise and fall of the dinosaurs and the dawning and flowering of the mammals. The most primitive of the extant conifers, the Araucarias, have very limited powers of dispersal over water but were formerly widespread on the continents of North and South America, Europe, Asia, Africa and Antarctica. Today we see a vestige of this formerly important group, three species in South America, two in Australia, one on Norfolk island, two in New Guinea and, quite remarkably, eight endemic species on New Caledonia, which lies at the extreme limit of the groups capacity for dispersal over water [2] (Fig. 5.1). The eight New Caledonian species cover as broad a range of morphology and ecological adaptation as does the rest of the genus put together. Sparse Auraucaria forests are found from the strand lines of the beaches right to the tops of the high mountains. These conifers provide a fine example of a group with limited means of dispersal which has undergone a spectacular adaptive radiation within the confines of a single island.

Our next example is a very different one, involving a highly mobile group of animals which have radiated on an extremely remote archipelago of islands.

5.2 The Honeycreepers of Hawaii

Even the modern air traveller cannot be but impressed by the awesome remoteness of the islands of Hawaii, nor by the bravery and fortitude of the ancient Polynesians who, in their open canoes, discovered and settled them. The chain of islands, one thousand miles long, lies in the central Pacific ocean two thousand miles from California to the east and two thousand miles north of the Marquesas group.

Not surprisingly, many groups of organisms have failed to reach and colonize these islands; there are no freshwater fish, no amphibians and reptiles, no land mammals and 21 orders of insects are absent. However, because of the isolation of the archipelago, many of the plants and animals which have successfully reached it have undergone spectacular radiations, for example (among the animals), the crickets, fruit-flies and carabid beetles; while 90% of the flora is endemic to the islands. To mention one group of plants in more detail, the lobeliads (Campanulaceae) included six endemic genera containing over 150 species.

Among the Hawaiian vertebrates the most impressive evolutionary divergence has occurred in an endemic family of birds, the Drepanididae or Hawaiian Honeycreepers. The family includes an array of arboreal seed, insect and nectar feeding species with a fabulous variety of specialised beaks and tongues (Fig. 5.2). The fame of this group is less than that of Darwin's finches living in the Galapagos islands [1, 4] but this is unwarranted, the extent and range of the Honeycreeper adaptive radiation is far greater.

Today we know of 23 species, in 11 endemic genera, one of which was

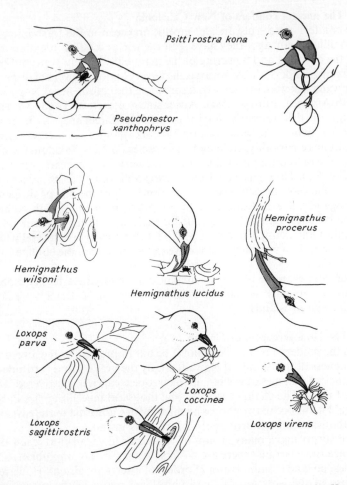

Fig. 5.2 The fabulous variety of bill-form and feeding habits among the Hawaiian Honeycreepers (redrawn from [2]).

discovered as late as 1974. All have been produced by speciation across the water gaps of the archipelago, from a single ancestral species probably blown to the islands by some distant hurricane. We shall never know the precise identity of this ancestor, but recent morphological studies by Raikow [5] argue strongly that it was a holarctic fringillid finch (Carduelinae). Such an ancestor would have had the typical broad, strong finch break and muscular tongue for feeding on hard seeds. Raikow has provided us with a speculative, but entirely plausible, phylogenetic tree which derives all the known drepanidid genera from this ancestral finch (Fig. 5.3). Still living today, there are two genera which are little modified from the ancestral founder; they still have finch-like

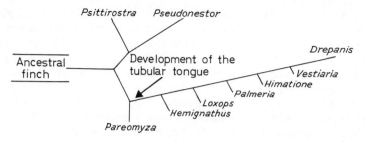

Fig. 5.3 A suggested evolutionary tree for the Hawaiian Drepanididae [5].

beaks and tongues. The species in the genus *Psittirostra* have short and conical beaks and seeds make up the bulk of their diet, augmented by some insect life (Fig. 5.2). In one species, *P. psittacea*, the upper mandible is somewhat parrot-like and it favours flowers, fruit and caterpillars. This particular line of beak adaptation is taken further in *Pseudonestor xanthrophrys* which lives in the forests of Maui. It uses its powerful bill to crush and to tear apart twigs and branches in a search for the wood-boring beetles on which it lives (Fig. 5.2).

However, the main line of evolution from the finch ancestor (Fig. 5.3) produced feeding specializations of a quite different nature. In the absence of competing passerines from abroad, the early drepanidids radiated into a wide variety of feeding niches. In general the bill became longer, narrower and more delicate and the tongue became elongated, as a specialization for feeding on insects. Today, *Paroreomyza maculata* represents this stage of evolution. Its long, stout beak is used to lever away bark from the trunk and branches of trees in its search for insects.

A second line of evolution has produced a series of forms adapted for feeding on nectar from flowers; they all have operculate nostrils and tubular tongues. The tongue narrows towards its tip and its lateral edges roll upwards and overlap thus forming a tube. Such a tongue is thought to take up nectar by capillarity, possibly aided by a sucking action of the mouth.

The four species of *Loxops* have short, thin beaks, which are straight or slightly decurved, and tubular tongues. They all take some nectar from shallow flowers but really are specialist insectivores. *L. virens* and *L. parva* forage for insects among foliage while *L. sagittirostris*, now sadly extinct, used its long and stout beak to probe for large insects in bark and rotting wood. The most specialized of the four is *L. coccinea*. In a remarkable convergence with the crossbills of the high north, the tips of its mandibles are crossed and the bones and muscles of its jaws asymmetric. The whole feeding apparatus is adapted for providing sideways leverage and is used to pry open buds and seed-heads, thus exposing hidden insects (Fig. 5.2).

Hemignathus species are larger than those of *Loxops* and have much

45

longer, decurved beaks. Besides taking nectar, with their tubular tongues, they also take insects. They climb trees and use their beaks as hammers, like woodpeckers, to drive out insects from the wood and bark. In *H. obscurus* the lower mandible is almost as long as the upper and the whole beak is used to probe for insects. In contrast *H. wilsoni*, from Hawaii, has a beak in which the upper part is long and decurved while the lower is short and straight (Fig. 5.2). The two mandibles perform quite different functions; the lower is used to lever insects out of bark and decaying wood, while the upper makes a fine, long probe. Both *H. procerus* and *H. lucidus* have long decurved beaks and specialize in taking nectar from the trumpet-like flowers of lobeliads, although again both have been observed using their beaks to probe decaying wood, and to sift through litter in a search for arthropods.

The genera *Palmeria*, *Vestiaria*, *Drepanis* and *Himatione* contain the most nectarivorous species, although again all take some insect life. Perhaps *Vestiaria coccinea* and the two extinct species of *Drepanis* represent the most specialized nectar feeders; all have or had, very long decurved beaks for probing the deep lobeliad flowers of the forest.

Two final genera are somewhat enigmatic and are difficult to relate to the rest of the family. *Ciridops anna*, the only species in its genus, lived in the forests of Hawaii but is now extinct. We know little of its way of life, indeed only five specimens were ever collected. Its beak was rather stout and finch-like, but it had a fully tubular tongue. If we are to regard a tongue adapted for taking nectar as an advanced characteristic, as Raikow argues, then the finch-like form of the beak must have been secondarily derived from a long, thin beak, an adaptation to the species diet of palm fruits.

Melamprosops phaesoma was only discovered in 1974, on the island of Maui, and we know very little about it. Its tongue is short, straight and stout but there are anatomical indications that is has been derived from a tubular type, although it is no longer used to take nectar.

On these isolated islands, which passerines manage to reach only very, very rarely, an ancestral finch has given rise to an endemic family adapted for the taking of nectar, insects and seeds, all of which are plentiful throughout the year in the Hawaiian forest. The different species are morphologically adapted for a wide range of feeding niches. In particular the relative importance of seeds, nectar and insects varies from species to species as do the plants and flowers exploited and the ways in which the insects are taken. It is these differences in foraging behaviour and in diet which have allowed various species to live in sympatry, in the same habitat, on the same island. When two closely related species, with similar but different ecological requirements invade an island and co-exist successfully, their differences in diet and morphology tend to become even greater. The result of this character displacement is to reduce competition between the two species.

The Honeycreepers provide a good example of this phenomenon. In the absence of related competitors, *Loxops virens* uses its tubular tongue to take nectar from a variety of shallow flowers and its short, straight beak to glean insects from the surfaces of leaves. On the island of Kauai it co-exists with *L. parva* which also has a short, straight, delicate beak used to take nectar and foliage insects. On this island, the beak of *L. virens* is unusually large and it feeds mainly on insects taken from the branches and trunks of trees. Clearly there has been displacement both of its diet and of its beak morphology.

In contrast, on the island of Hawaii *L. virens* co-existed with *L. sagittirostris*, a species with a long, heavy and stout beak, which fed on insects. Here *L. virens* showed displacement in the opposite direction; it had an unusually short and delicate beak and concentrated on nectar as its major food source.

5.3 Unresolved problems
While problems of dispersal are undoubtably important in determining whether a group shall or shall not radiate, other factors must play a part. Several groups of animals right at the limits of their dispersal abilities are conspicuous in their failure to radiate; frogs in Fiji and New Zealand, insectivores in the Greater Antilles, mammals in the Solomons, snakes in Fiji and lizards in Samoa. In Hawaii, the Drepanidids have produced a dazzling array of species but other successful colonists, a crow, honeyeaters, fly-catchers and a warbler have all failed to do so.

The reasons for these failures have never been satisfactorily explained. It may be that the groups involved are relatively recent arrivals, although there is no evidence to support this. Some islands may not provide sufficient ecological variability for the co-existence of a range of sympatric species. Some groups may retain their powers of dispersal, thus negating the possibility of genetic isolation of populations and of speciation. Finally, in some situations the adaptive radiation of an early immigrant may prevent the diversification of a later one with similar requirements. Thus the early adaptive radiation of the Hawaiian Drepanidids may have filled the available nectar-eating niches and thus pre-empted the Australian Honeyeaters who arrived later.

References
[1] Bowman, R. I. (1961), *Univ. Calif. Berkeley Publ. Zool.*, **58**, 1–302.
[2] Carlquist, S. (1974), *Island Biology*, Columbia University Press, New York.
[3] Diamond, J. M. (1974), *Systematic Zool.*, **26**, 263–268.
[4] Lack, D., (1947), *Darwin's Finches*, Cambridge University Press, Cambridge.
[5] Raikow, R. J. (1976), *The Living Bird*, Cornell Laboratory of Ornithology, Ithaca NY.

6 Some dangers of living
on an island

The fate of most populations is eventual extinction, but island species appear to be particularly susceptible. For example, of the 94 species of birds which are known to have become extinct since 1600 only 9 lived on continents, the rest were endemic to islands. To see the full enormity of this we must remember that island species make up only 10% of the world's avifauna.

Island populations will always be more vulnerable than continental ones because of their smaller size and restricted range. For this reason they have been particularly hard hit by man's activities, by his hunting, his destruction of habitat and by his introduction of predators, diseases and alien competitors. In New Zealand the role of large grazer was filled not by ruminant mammals but by large flightless birds, the moas. By the time Captain Cook arrived, in the late 1700s, the Polynesian Maoris had hunted to extinction at least 20 species of these magnificent giants. Today none remains. Again, in Fiji the introduction of the mongoose had eliminated the barred-wing rail *Nesoclopeus poecilopterus* from Viti Levu within 100 years [1].

The impact of man is not the only factor at work however. It fails to explain why, for example, in Fiji, the parrot-finch *Erythrura cyanovirens* is common and widespread while its relative *E. kleinschmidti* is on the brink of extinction, even though its montane forest habitat is practically undisturbed. Nor why the long-legged warbler *Trichocichla rufa* has become extinct in recent times while the closely related Fiji warbler *Viti ruficapilla* is a common bird of the rainforest. Clearly extinction of island species is not a simple matter, some species are more likely candidates for doom than are others, whatever the direction that it comes.

6.1 The taxon cycle
There is increasing evidence that when a species invades an island from a source area, it has started on a sequence of evolutionary changes which will eventually increase the probability of its own extinction. During this series of events, which in analogy with the life cycle of an individual organism has been termed a taxon cycle [5], a species spreads and diversifies but then declines and finally becomes extinct. the process, which has been observed in ants and birds [2, 4, 5], is most clearly seen in long chains of islands receiving colonists from a source area. For example, in the West Indies, which are colonized from North, Central and South America, Ricklefs and Cox [4] have been able to assign

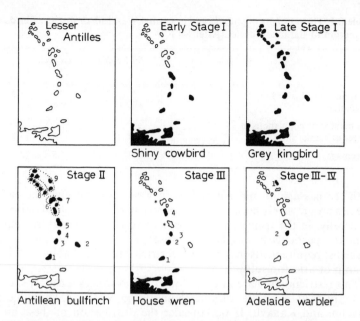

Fig. 6.1 The progressive stages of the taxon cycle exemplified by several birds of the Lesser Antilles. The small figures indicate subspecies. The House Wren has become extinct on the islands marked* within the present century (after [4])

species to 4 arbitrary stages of the taxon cycle, based on geographical distribution and the degree of sub-speciation. The stages, which represent a temporal sequence through which all invading species may eventually pass, are: (I) species which have relatively recently invaded the archipelago, they are widespread or spreading and show little or no sub-speciation on different islands; (II) older invasions, species whose dispersal abilities have, for some reason, been reduced, and who because of their genetic isolation show considerable sub-speciation; (III) Species with many sub-species but in which extinctions on various islands are leading to a fragmented distribution, a process which culminates at stage (IV), species endemic to single islands. The geographical ranges of species presently at each of these stages are shown in Fig. 6.1.

Ricklefs and Cox show quite clearly that as species move through the taxon cycle their chance of extinction is progressively increased (Table 6.1).

The central problem is that of why, following a phase of expansion and differentiation, an island species declines towards extinction. The reason appears to be that as a species moves through the cycle its population size gradually decreases. We saw earlier that colonizing species occupy coastal or secondary habitats on mainlands. As they expand on to islands they initially occupy a broad range of habitat including many from which they are absent on the mainland. However,

Table 6.1 The numbers of endangered or extinct West Indian species of birds as a function of the taxon cycle. (After [4])

	Stages of the taxon cycle			
	I	*II*	*III*	*IV*
Total number of island populations	428	289	229	57
The number of populations in danger or extinct since 1850	0	8	12	13
Percentage	0	3	5	23

with the passage of millenia and as they progress through the cycle, species progressively become restricted to a narrower range of habitats. Generally, in the tropics, species become restricted to mature, stable habitats, particularly montane rainforest [2, 3], although those with specialist requirements may become restricted to other habitats such as swamp or arid forest [4].

This restriction in habitat use by older island species is clearly shown by the birds living on the volcanic islands of Fiji, Viti Levu, Vanua Levu, Taveuni and Kadavu. If we consider the distribution of these birds across the Pacific we can allocate them to same cycle stages used by Ricklefs and Cox. To obtain a measure of the utilization of habitats in Fiji by species at different stages of the cycle we can proceed as follows. First consider each Stage I species, individually and in turn. If a species uses only one habitat we can allocate the habitat a score of 1. If it uses 2 habitats each receives 0.5, three habitats 0.33 and so on. If we do this for each Stage I species, each habitat will receive a total score which can then be expressed as a percentage of the total of all habitat scores. The percentages that result are a simple measure of the relative use made of each habitat by Stage I species. We can then do a similar analysis for species at the other stages of the cycle (Fig. 6.2).

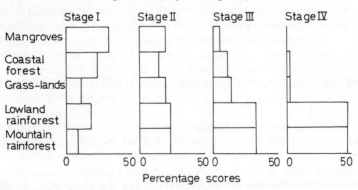

Fig. 6.2 The use made of the habitats of the Fijian islands by birds at different stages of the taxon cycle. See text for further details.

Table 6.2 The rate of capture of birds in Fiji as a function of habitat and taxon cycle stage. A net-day is a standard catching effort based on 60 nets erected for one day.

	Number of individuals caught per net-day per species in:		
	Coastal habitats	Lowland forest	Montane forest
Stage I species	1.11	0.92	0.67
Stage II species	1.32	0.61	0.87
Stage III species	0.53	0.34	0.21
Stage IV species		0.11	0.04

Such an analysis reveals a clear tendency for species to become restricted in habitat as the cycle proceeds, the Stage IV endemics being largely restricted to rainforest. At the same time there is evidence, from the rate at which I caught birds in nets, that the restriction in habitat use is accompanied by a decrease in population densities.

Table 6.2 shows for different habitats, and for different stages of the taxon cycle, the mean numbers of individuals caught per species per unit catching effort. The data indicate that for each stage of the taxon cycle mean population densities are highest in coastal vegetation and lowest in montane forest. If we consider individual habitats it is also clear that Stage I species have the highest population densities and Stage IV species the lowest.

The overall effect is a reduction in population size and an increase in the chance of extinction, through habitat destruction, predation or random fluctuation, as the species moves through the taxon cycle.

The introduction of predators, or the destruction of a habitat such as rainforest, will accelerate a natural course of events. The tragedy is that the effect will be greatest on Stage IV island endemics and least on the widely distributed and common Stage I and II species. The implications for conservation are clear.

6.2 What drives the cycle?

Ricklefs and Cox argue that the cycle is driven from without, that competitors, species with similar ecological requirements, force species through the cycle. They argue that successful, new immigrants have a distinct competitive advantage over species that have been on an island for long periods. The living environment of the island, potential predators, diseases, parasites, competitors and food organisms, have had little exposure to the newcomer. Consequently, the productivity of the immigrant population is not greatly inhibited by the biotic environment and it becomes widespread across most habitats.

Progressively, however, the newcomer becomes an important part of the island community and the rest of the biotic environment adjusts, by evolutionary changes, to exploit it or to avoid exploitation by it. This counter-adaptation reduces the relative competitive ability and productivity of the immigrant species.

If now, other immigrant species arrive on the island they in turn will be at an advantage and the older established species will become restricted to those habitats in which it can compete most effectively.

This sequence of events is speculative but plausible. Empirical evidence for the proposed reduction in competitive ability due to counter-adaptation will depend upon detailed field work and the experimental manipulation of simpler systems.

References

[1] Gorman, M. L. (1975), *J. Zool.*, **175**, 273–278.
[2] Greenslade, P. J. M. (1968), *Evolution*, **22**, 751–761.
[3] Ricklefs, R. E. (1970), *Evolution*, **24**, 475–477.
[4] Ricklefs, R. E. & Cox, G. W. (1972), *Am. Nat.*, **106**, 195–219.
[5] Wilson, E. O. (1961), *Am. Nat.*, **95**, 169–193.

7 Continental habitat islands

So far we have been largely concerned with real islands surrounded by water. However, areas of habitats on continents may be just as effectively isolated from each other as are true islands, except that they are separated, not by water, but by expanses of inhospitable vegetation, which plants and animals adapted to other habitats cross only with varying degrees of difficulty. Habitats which are distributed in such an insular manner, and which have their own specialist biota, include desert oases, sphagnum bogs, the boreal regions found near the tops of high mountains and even individual plant species.

The theory of island biogeography formulated by MacArthur and Wilson in 1963 [4] was a landmark in biogeography and the following 15 years have seen great advances in our understanding of island patterns, most of them based on the predictions made by their equilibrium model. Unfortunately, diversity patterns on continents are not so easily studied and consequently our analysis of them is much less advanced [2].

However, those continental communities which are clearly insular in their distribution show gross differences in their isolation and patterns of immigration and extinction and some progress has been made in applying the equilibrium model to them. It must be recognized, however, that the majority of continental habitats form very complex mosaics and that in their case any insularity is obscure, and different analytical approaches will be required.

Given these restrictions we can now go on to look at several case studies where habitats have been treated as islands.

You will remember from Chapter 3 that according to the dynamic equilibrium model, the number of species on an island is correlated with and is a function of its area and its distance from a source of colonists. These two variables affect the rates of extinction of established species and the immigration of new species respectively. In Chapter 3 we discussed the effects of island area at some length and now, before looking at habitat islands, we must set the scene a little further by looking more closely at the effects of island remoteness. We might best do this by using the example MacArthur and Wilson used in their original paper [4]. They plotted the numbers of land and fresh-water birds living on the various islands of the Mollucas, Melanesia, Micronesia and Polynesia against island area. The result was a plot with a great deal of scatter due to the great variation in the distances of the various island from the source area of New Guinea (Fig. 7.1.). The different effects on species number of island area and distance from

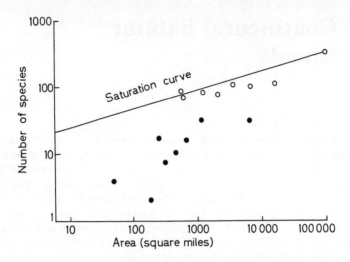

Fig. 7.1 The numbers of land and fresh-water birds living on the islands of the tropical Pacific, plotted against island area. The saturation curve is drawn through New Guinea, the source island, and the nearby but much smaller Kei Islands. The open circles represent islands near to New Guinea and the closed ones more distant islands [4].

source they separated by simply drawing a line through New Guinea and the nearby, but much smaller, Kei islands. This line, or saturation curve, describes the number of species that would be found on islands of various sizes if distances from the source was not a problem. You will see that islands near to New Guinea do indeed fall near to this line (open circles in Fig. 7.1), while more distant islands fall at various levels below the line. The 'percentage saturation' for any island can be calculated by expressing the number of species on the island as a percentage of the number one would find on a hypothetical island of the same size but

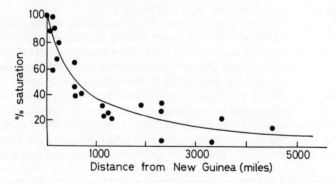

Fig. 7.2 The percentage saturation of Pacific island avifaunas (the number of species on an island expressed as a percentage of the number one would expect to find on an island of equal size but lying on the saturation curve) as a function of their distance from New Guinea [4].

lying on the saturation curve, near to the source. If such percentage saturation values are plotted against the island's distance from New Guinea the result is an exponential decline with increasing distance, as one would predict from the equilibrium model (Fig. 7.2).

We are now in a better position to consider some examples of habitat islands and to see how they compare with real oceanic ones.

7.1 Islands of Páramo vegetation

The first case study takes us to the high mountain peaks of the Andes of Venezuela, Columbia and Ecuador. Above the tree line, at some 3000 m, these mountains are covered with a typical vegetation consisting largely of dense tussocks of grass and known as páramo. These variously sized vegetation islands are separated by seas of wet montane forest on the lower slopes of the mountains (Fig. 7.3). The avifauna of these islands in the sky has been studied by Vuilleumier [8] and the flora by Simpson [6].

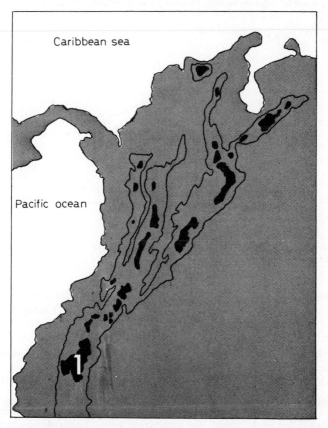

Fig. 7.3 The Northern Andes with islands of Páramo vegetation shown in black and the 1000 m contour shown by a continuous line. Island 1 is thought to be the source area for the birds living on the islands [8].

55

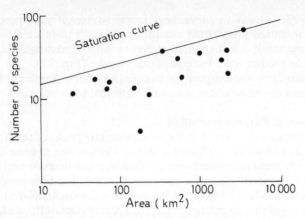

Fig. 7.4 The number of bird species found on Páramo islands of various areas. The saturation curve is drawn between Páramo 1 and its nearest neighbour [8].

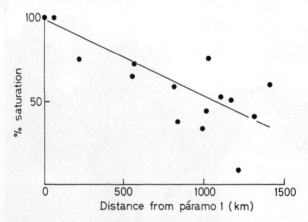

Fig. 7.5 The percentage saturation of the Páramo island avifaunas plotted against distance from the source area Páramo 1 [8].

The history of the avifauna is well documented and indicates an origin in the south and a faunal flow to the north. The large Páramo island in the south, labelled one in Fig. 7.3, can therefore be regarded as the source area.

In the sense that island faunas show a positive correlation with island area and an inverse correlation with distance from source, the páramo islands are acting as a true archipelago. Species diversity is correlated with island area, and the slope of the regression line (Z) at 0.29 falls within the range for true islands (Fig. 7.4). When saturation values are calculated for each island, the saturation curve being drawn between Páramo 1 and the nearest island and plotted against distance from source, there is a clear distance effect (Fig. 7.5). The evidence is that species numbers on these islands do represent equilibria between recurrent immigration and extinction.

The major difference between the Páramo islands and true islands is that of the shape of the distance-effect curve (Fig. 7.5), which is rectilinear as compared to the exponential curve of the Pacific island birds. Vuilleumier argues that this is because the isolation between real islands is more absolute than that between habitat islands. An exhausted bird falling into the sea will invariably die, but one falling into a different vegetation may well be able to rest and refuel.

Turning to the flora of the Páramos, species number is again positively correlated to island area, but the relationship is only weak (Fig. 7.6). For a better relationship we must go back in time several 1000 years. During the Pleistocene glaciations the climate in the Andes was much cooler and the tree-line descended some 1500 m below its modern level. Consequently the Páramo islands were much larger than they are now. If we plot the number of species of plants living on each island today against the area of the same island some 10 000 years ago, the positive correlation becomes much stronger (Fig. 7.6). Simpson concludes from this that plants colonized the Páramos during glacial times when immigration was much easier because the islands were larger and closer together. Our modern islands, shadows of their former selves, are supersaturated with species, holding numbers of species more appropriate to their Pleistocene sizes than to their contemporary ones. With the passage of time the islands will be losing species by extinction as they relax towards the 'correct' equilibrium number consistent with their present areas. Such a decline in species diversity following a reduction in island size has happened fairly rapidly in various vertebrate faunas, as we shall see in Chapter 8. That it has not happened so quickly in the case of the Páramo

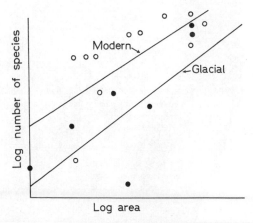

Fig. 7.6 The relationship between the areas of various Páramo islands and the number of plant species each supports. The open circles represent the areas of the islands today and the closed circles their areas during the Pleistocene glaciations [6].

flora is probably due to the relatively long life-span of most plants and their high population densities as compared to most vertebrates.

7.2 Mountain mammals

For the second study we stay among the mountain tops but move north, to the Great Basin of North America. Much of Nevada and areas of Utah and California are covered by a hot, dry sea of sage-brush desert out of which isolated mountain peaks soar to over 10 000 feet. The cool boreal habitats, characteristic of the upper slopes of these mountains, support a community of mountain mammals which came originally from the Sierra Nevada to the west and the Rockies to the east, and which are quite unable to survive in the desert below (Fig. 7.7).

Brown [1] has studied the distribution of 15 of these mammals on 17 montane islands of pinon-juniper woodland and meadow. Again the number of species is positively correlated to island area with a regression line of slope (Z) 0.43. Four comparable areas on the Sierra Nevada mainland have more species and a species-area curve of much lower slope ($Z = 0.12$) (Fig. 7.8). These relationships are similar to those for animals living on real islands and mainlands, but you will probably have been struck by the very high Z value of 0.43.

You will recall that areas of mainland have a lower slope to the species-area curve than do a series of islands because the islands have much lower rates of immigration. The lower the rate of immigration the higher the value of Z. This would suggest that the present rate of immigration of boreal mammals to the montane islands of the Great Basin is very low.

On the oceanic islands where recurrent colonization is the order of the

Fig. 7.7 The Great Basin with its mountain-top islands, shown in black, lying between the hatched Sierra Nevada to the left and the Rocky Mountains to the right [1].

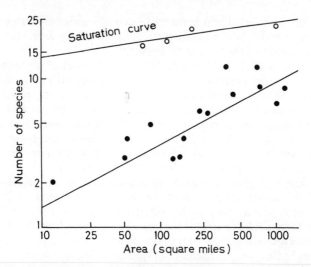

Fig. 7.8 The number of species of boreal mammals living on the montane islands of the Great Basin as a function of their areas. The saturation curve is drawn through four areas (open circles) of the Sierra Nevada mainland [1].

day, there is a clear, inverse correlation between the percentage saturation of an island's biota and its distance from the source (Fig. 7.2). When the percentage saturation of each of the montane islands in the Great Basin is plotted against distance to the nearest of the two sources, no relationship can be seen (Fig. 7.9).

Brown concluded from this evidence that these boreal mammal faunas

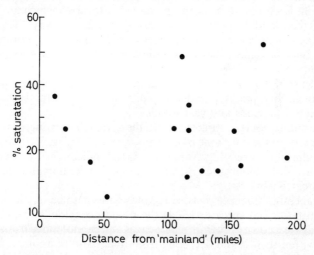

Fig. 7.9 The percentage saturation of the boreal mammal faunas of the Great Basin plotted against distance from one of the two source areas of the Sierra Nevada or Rocky Mountains, whichever is the closer [1].

do not represent equilibria between recurrent immigration and extinction; the present rate of immigration is effectively zero, the desert providing an absolute barrier to dispersal.

To seek how the animals reached the mountains at all we must again go back to the Pleistocene. Then the pinon-juniper wooodlands descended to some 2000 feet below their present level, providing a contiguous distribution of forest across the Great Basin. Thus up to 10 000 years ago, mammals now restricted to the mountain tops ranged freely across the whole area. At the end of the Pleistocene, as the climate changed and the woodland retreated up the mountains, the boreal mammals became trapped on their heavenly islands.

Since the isolation of the montane islands, extinctions, related to the sizes of the different islands and the maximum populations they can hold, have gradually reduced the faunal diversity. We know this for sure because fossil evidence tells us that species once inhabited islands from which they are now absent. Some 8000 years later the largest islands still have almost their original number of species while even the smallest have one or two. This suggests that the reduction of species number to the equilibria appropriate to the present low rate of immigration is a slow process. We shall return to this problem in the next chapter.

This study of boreal mammals makes an interesting contrast with the previous one on boreal birds, for they were quite capable of crossing barriers between their habitat islands.

7.3 Caves of limestone
In the Greenbrier valley of West Virginia there are a number of limestone exposures set in a sea of other, non-cavernous rocks (Fig. 7.10) [3]. Each limestone island is riddled with caves which are linked, within the island, by subterranean passages and waterways. Thus cave-dwelling species can move within an area of limestone with comparative ease, but movement between different exposures is fraught with difficulty.

At least 18 terrestrial and 12 aquatic cave-limited species live in the area, including spiders, pseudoscorpions, insects, a decapod crustacean, amphipods, isopods and gastropods.

The number of terrestrial species in the caves (S) is strongly influenced by the area of the limestone island ($S = 0.18A^{0.72}$) (Fig. 7.10). Again we are dealing with a very high value of Z. Is this indicative of very low rates of recurrent recolonization, as was the case for the boreal mammals of the Great Basin?

In fact migration rates between islands do seem to be very low, indeed several terrestrial species such as the pseudoscorpion *Kleptochthonius orpheus* are known only from single caves and cannot move from cave to cave within their island, let alone from one island to another. It is the experience of cave ecologists that terrestrial cave species are rarely found near the mouths of caves, which makes migration between islands unlikely.

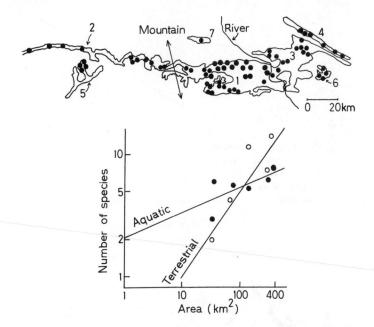

Fig. 7.10 Limestone islands in the Greenbrier Valley. The seven islands are isolated from each other by areas of other rock types, by Droop mountain and by the Greenbrier river. Caves in the limestone are indicated by the closed circles. The lower figure shows the numbers of terrestrial and aquatic invertebrates living in the islands as a function of their areas [3].

The aquatic animals of the Greenbrier caves have a very different pattern of distribution with no significant correlation between species number and island area ($S = 2.14A^{0.19}$; Fig. 7.10). This type of distribution, very like that found on different areas of a mainland, is highly suggestive of a high rate of exchange of aquatic species between the limestone islands. In support of this, Culver and his colleagues have found that the aquatic species are often common in the drip pools at the cave entrances and that many can move through the sub-surface water of the ground between the limestone islands.

So here we have two groups of species, living on the same islands, but whose patterns of distribution are very different due to their different powers of dispersal.

7.4 Gold mines and Pikas
Our final case study is particularly interesting because it is an attempt to apply MacArthur and Wilson's Theory of Island Biogeography not to island communities, but to island populations of a single species.

Pikas (Fig. 7.11) are North American lagomorphs which look rather like diminutive tail-less rabbits. They are creatures of weathered cliffs in

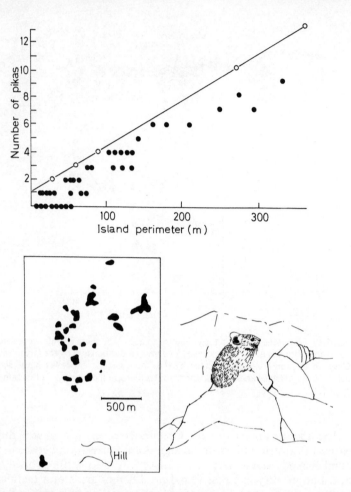

Fig. 7.11 The number of Pikas found on islands formed from piles of rocks as a function of island area. The saturation curve is drawn through the most saturated islands. The map shows the spacing of the mine tailings, which form the islands, at Bodie in California [7].

the Rocky Mountains and Pacific coast ranges, and typically make their territorial homes in piles of broken rock.

Smith [7] has studied the Rocky Mountain Pika *Ochotona princeps* in an unusual habitat, in Bodie, an old Sierra Nevada ghost town, surrounded by the tailings of abandoned gold-mines. These tailings, each an island of boulders in a sea of sagebrush, differ markedly in size and lie at differing distances from each other, while two particularly large piles might be regarded as mainlands.

The abundance of Pikas on the boulder islands is related to the size of the island, measured at its perimeter where most of the animals live (Fig. 7.11). If a saturation line is drawn through the most crowded islands it is apparent that most contain fewer species than they could theoretically hold. Indeed 40% of the islands supported no Pikas at all (Fig. 7.11).

The populations living on the mine tailings apparently represent equilibria between extinctions, which are directly related to island size, and recolonization which is an inverse function of inter-island distance.

In *The Theory of Island Biogeography*, MacArthur and Wilson [5] used birth and death rates to describe the probable fluctuations of small populations and to calculate their expected survival time. The probable time to extinction (E) is related to the size of the population and is described by

$$E = (1/K\lambda)(\lambda/\mu)^K$$

where λ is the per capita birth rate, μ the per capita death rate and K the maximum population the island can support.

Using this formula, and armed with a knowledge of Pika demography at Bodie, Smith calculates that islands with a K value of more than 4 may be expected to last for some hundreds of years but that populations with a K of 2 will be likely to become extinct in under 10 years. It is not surprising then to find that the uninhabited islands all have K values of less than 3 (Fig. 7.11). The problem remains as to why they are not rapidly recolonized. At Bodie, dispersal of the year's young takes place late in the season when temperatures are high and dispersal is least likely to be successful. Even islands close to a source of propagules may be empty but the proportion of unoccupied islands increases with distance from the mainlands or other occupied islands (Table 7.1).

Thus when an island population does become extinct, and this must happen frequently because of the number of small islands, the island may remain empty for a long period because the chances of it being recolonized are low. The sagebrush desert acts as a very effective barrier against dispersal.

Table 7.1 The percentage of unoccupied islands for movements of increasing distance to the nearest source of colonists [7].

Distance to the nearest occupied island (m)	% of islands unoccupied
0–100	28
101–200	33
201–300	63
301–400	75
401–450	100

References

[1] Brown, J. H. (1971), *Am. Nat.*, **105**, 467–478.

[2] Cody, M. L. & Diamond, J. M. (eds) (1975), *Ecology and Evolution of Communities*, Belknap Press, Cambridge, Mass.

[3] Culver, D., Holsinger, J. R. & Baroody, (1973), *Evolution*, **27**, 689–695.

[4] MacArthur, R. H. & Wilson, E. O. (1963), *Evolution*, **17**, 373–387.

[5] MacArthur, R. H. & Wilson, E. O. (1967), *The Theory of Island Biogeography*, Princeton University Press, Princeton.

[6] Simpson, B. B. (1974), *Science*, **185**, 698–700.

[7] Smith, A. T. (1974), *Ecology*, **55**, 1112–1119.

[8] Vuilleumier, F. (1970), *Am. Nat.*, **104**, 373–388.

8 Island ecology and nature reserves

As man continues to modify the vegetation of the world to his own needs the survival of many species of plants and animals will be possible only in reserves of natural habitat. These will often be small areas erected in a desperate attempt to save some endangered species with a specialized habitat requirement, or perhaps a traditional, colonial breeding place. However in the long term the preservation of complete, mature communities of plants and animals holds the most promise for coming generations of humans. Time is fast running out for the preservation of areas of some habitats, particularly the tropical rain-forests of West Africa and South-east Asia.

'The balance of advantage would appear to be strongly in favour of felling and selling, as much as possible, as soon as possible.' Fiji Department of Forestry Policy Proposals 1971.

For the preservation of such intact communities much larger areas will be required, particularly if the large, far-ranging animals high up the trophic ladder are to survive. Such natural reserves, by their very nature, will be islands in an inhospitable sea of man-modified vegetation or urban sprawl. Because of this, various authors [4, 5, 6] have suggested that studies of insular biogeography and ecology should be of value in the rational design and management of wildlife reserves. We might pose three pertinent questions.

8.1 How many species will a reserve support?
We have already seen (Chapter 3) that the number of species living at a particular location is related to area; islands support fewer species than do similar areas of a mainland, and small islands have fewer species than do large ones. This applies not only to real islands but also to habitat islands; Fig. 8.1 shows the number of bird species living in British forests of various sizes.

If we destroy the greater part of a vast belt of natural forest, leaving just a small reserve, initially it will be supersaturated with species, containing more than is appropriate to its area when at equilibrium. Since the population sizes of the species living in the forest will now be much reduced, the extinction rate will increase, for the reasons we discussed in Chapter 3, and the number of species will decline towards equilibrium. This is of course in contrast to what happens on oceanic islands where equilibrium is approached from below.

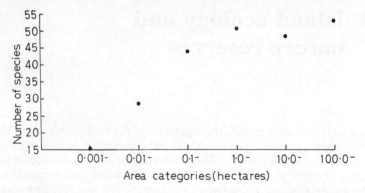

Fig. 8.1 The number of species of birds living in British woods of various size categories [7].

What will be the extent of this reduction in species? Using Darling-ton's rough rule of thumb we can predict that if we were to destroy 90% of the Fijian rainforest, leaving the 10% in a single reserve, we would lose 50% of the forest species. Destruction of 99% would lead to the loss of 75%.

We need not restrict ourselves to rules of thumb, however; nature has carried out an experiment which indicates that such loss really does occur. During the last ice-age much of the world's water was bound up in ice and the level of the sea was some 100–200 m lower than it is today. Islands which are now separated from their mainland by water less than 100 m deep actually formed part of that mainland up to 10 000 years ago. Such land-bridge islands include Great Britain, Ireland and Guernsey lying off mainland Europe, Tasmania off Australia, Japan off Asia, Sri lanka off India and Sumatra, Java and Borneo off South-east Asia. These islands originally shared a species-rich fauna and flora with the continent to which they were attached. When 10 000 years ago, the glaciers melted and the seas rose, the islands were cut off with a super-saturated fauna and flora inappropriate to their size. Gradually species have been lost by an excess of extinction over immigration. This is quite apparent in Java where, for example, a number of mammals known to be present during the ice-age are now absent; the Orangutan, several large cats, a hyaena, bears, the hippopotamus, tapirs, antelopes, and wild cattle.

Trinidad, a land-bridge island formerly attached to south America, still contains more species of reptiles and amphibians than do oceanic islands of similar area, despite the passage of 10 000 years (Fig. 3.1). Diamond [3] has carried out surveys on various land-bridge islands off New Guinea to see how far they have relaxed towards equilibrium in 10 000 years. The larger islands with areas above a few hundred square miles still have more species of lowland birds than do islands at equilibrium, but considerably less than does New Guinea itself

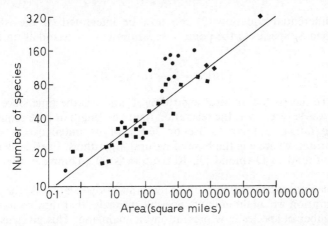

Fig. 8.2 The number of species of land-birds living in the lowland rainforest on small islands off New Guinea, plotted as a function of island area. The squares represent islands which have not had a land connection to New Guinea and whose avifaunas are at equilibrium. The regression line is fitted through these points. The circles represent former land-bridge islands connected to New Guinea some 10 000 years ago. Note that the large ones have more species than one would expect for their size [3].

(Fig. 8.2). They have lost some excess species but not all. In contrast, small former land-bridge islands, under one hundred square miles in area, have the same number of species as do oceanic islands; they have lost all their excess in under 10 000 years.

8.2 How long does it take to lose species?

We have an indication from Diamond's study of New Guinea satellite islands that loss of species will be faster on small islands or reserves, and will be much slower on large ones. This is as we would expect from the equilibrium model; large islands will hold large populations with low extinction rates and relaxation to equilibrium will be prolonged.

It is possible to make reasonably accurate estimates of the time required for a supersaturated fauna or flora to relax its equilibrium.

If the island has more species than it should at equilibrium the change in the number of species per year will be given by

$$\frac{dS_t}{dt} = I - E \tag{1}$$

where S_t is the number of species on the island at time t, and I and E are the total annual immigration and extinction rates.

Now refer back to Equation 3 in Chapter 3 in order to satisfy yourself that

$$\frac{dS_t}{dt} = \lambda P - (\lambda + \mu)S_t \tag{2}$$

67

This differential equation (2) can now be integrated. If the island contained S_0 species at the point of separation of the island at time t_0, then

$$tr = t/[\ln(S_0 - \hat{S}) - \ln(S_t - \hat{S})] \tag{3}$$

where ln means the 'natural logarithm of' and t is the time since the island was severed. tr is the relaxation time, the length of time required for the fauna to relax to $1/e$ or 36.8% of its initial excess over equilibrium, where e is the base of natural logarithms. Further details can be found in Diamond [3]. Relaxation is 90% complete after 2.3 relaxation times.

We can now apply this formula to real land-bridge islands. At the time of separation we might assume, possible wrongly, that they contained the number of species now present on the mainland. This gives us the value S_0 to feed into Equation 3. The expected equilibrium value $\hat{S}$ we can calculate from the species-area curve of oceanic islands in the vicinity. S_t is the number of species presently on the island and t we can take as 10 000 years. Using this approach, Diamond [5] has calculated relaxation times for 134 species of lowland New Guinea birds stranded on former land-bridge islands (Table 8.1). As predicted, the relaxation times increase with increasing island size.

Relaxation times will vary from taxon to taxon. Case [2] has calculated values for lizards living on the land-bridge islands of the Gulf of California (Table 8.1) and finds them higher then those published for birds. This he argues is due to lizards living at higher population densities than other homeotherms and thus having lower extinction rates.

In the above studies it was assumed that all the land-bridge islands became isolated 10 000 years ago. In fact the time of separation for different islands varied from 6000 to 14 000 years ago due to the gradual rise of sea-level. Wilcox [12] has demonstrated a quantitative relationship between the length of time for which various islands in the

Table 8.1 Relaxation times for birds and lizards living on former land-bridge islands. (From [2] and [5])

Island group and taxon	Island area (km^2)	tr (years)
Forest birds:	7 800	9 000
Satellite islands	1 630	9 150
off New Guinea	450	6 100
	140	2 630
	1	≪ 1 000
Lizards:	1 196	13 200
Gulf of	67	9 500
California	5	≪ 10 000

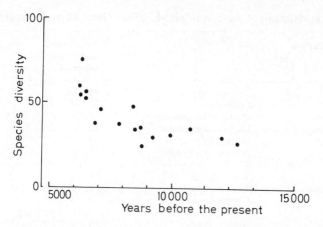

Fig. 8.3 The diversity of lizard species on former land-bridge islands plotted as a function of the length of time for which they have been isolated [12].

Gulf of California have been separated and the number of species of lizards they contain, having made corrections for the effects of island size and latitude (Fig. 8.3). The value of his work is that it provides direct evidence of the loss of species with time and does not rely on assumptions about the number of species present at the point of separation nor about the expected number at equilibrium, both of which may be open to question.

8.3 Which species will be lost?

In general, species living at low population densities will be at greatest risk of becoming extinct, due to population fluctuations. Such species include those with very large range requirements, those high up the trophic ladder and those which can live only in rare habitats.

During the cool climate of the Pleistocene, the Great Basin of North America was covered by a vegetation now confined to the summits of the mountains in the area. At the end of the Pleistocene the low-altitude vegetation began to change to arid scrub and desert, leaving 13 species of mammals trapped high on the mountains.

Over the last 10 000 years, these species have been subject to continuing extinction but have received no immigrants. Brown [1] has shown clearly that the carnivores, high up the trophic scale and living at low densities, have survived on fewer 'islands' than have the common herbivores (Table 8.2).

As we would expect, the carnivores are restricted to the largest 'islands' of woodland where they can maintain relatively large populations. The specialized herbivores, with a need for rare habitats, have fared worst of all and are now found on very few 'islands'.

Again, if we return to the lizards of the Gulf of California [2], we find that those most prone to extinction are not a random subset of the

Table 8.2 Mammals of the boreal 'islands' of the Great Basin. (After [1])

Diet and habitat	Species	No. of wood-land 'islands' inhabited	Average
Herbivores present in wide variety of habitats	Neotoma cinerea	14	
	Eutamias umbrinus	14	
	Spermophilus lateralis	13	11.6
	Microtus longicaudus	12	
	Marmota flaviventer	9	
	Thamomys talpoides	8	
Carnivores	Sorex vagrans	6	
	Sorex palustris	6	5
	Mustela erminea	3	
Herbivores with specialist habitat needs	Zapus princeps	4	
	Ochotona princeps	4	
	Spermophilus beldingi	3	3
	Lepus townsendi	1	

species pool. They follow the familiar pattern: *Coleonyx variegatus* and *Streptosaurus mearnsi* are habitat specialists on rocky outcrops, while *Xantusia vigilis* is an extreme habitat specialist occurring only in decaying cactus. Two species in the genus *Crotaphytus* are carnivores living on smaller lizards.

8.4 The design of reserves

Nature reserves, as habitat islands, are influenced by the same factors as real islands; final species number will be related to area and will be a resultant of differential immigration and extinction rates. However, while real islands are usually adjacent to rich source areas, from which they receive immigrants, nature reserves will often not be. Progressively, as more and more vegetation is altered, reserves of mature habitat will become completely isolated. As on land-bridge islands the dominant process in a nature reserve will be that of species extinction. That is not to say that immigration will not take place, it will. But it will involve the common 'weedy' species that thrive in the man-dominated habitats surrounding the reserves, and not the species of mature habitats for whom the reserve was established.

It is the task, therefore, of the reserve architect to do everything he can to reduce the probability of extinctions resultant on reduced population sizes.

What lessons can he learn from studies of insular biogeography?

The message coming over loud and very clear is that reserves should be as large as we can make them. A large reserve will support more species at equilibrium by allowing the existence of larger populations with lower extinction rates. The minimum size (it is difficult to imagine how one could be *too* big) will vary from locality to locality and will depend upon the community one wishes to preserve. As a general guideline Sullivan and Schaffer [10] have suggested that community reserves will be adequate if they are large enough to support populations of large mammals; in many parts of the world thousands of square kilometres will be necessary for this. Barro Colarado, a 1500 ha island formed by the building of the Panama canal, has lost 15 species of birds since 1914 [11]. On the New Guinea islands described earlier, 32 lowland species of birds have been lost from all the land-bridge islands, some as large as 8000 km². Few reserves of even this size are likely to be set aside in the tropical rainforest.

The landscape is not homogeneous, but is a mosaic of successional patches of habitat. A reserve should be large enough to contain a normal pattern of successional changes resultant on disturbance by fire, wind and the death of old trees [8], particularly as these can act as internal sources of recolonization. It is also important to know the timing and

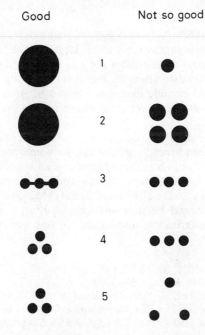

Fig. 8.4 A set of general design rules for nature reserves based on theories of island biogeography. The designs on the left are preferable to those on the right because they should enjoy lower rates of species extinction. (1) A large reserve will hold larger populations with lower probabilities of going extinct than will a small reserve. (2) A single reserve is preferable to a series of smaller reserves of equal total area, since these will support only small populations with relatively high probabilities of going extinct. (3–5) If reserves must be fragmented, then they should be connected by corridors of similar vegetation or be placed equidistant and as near to each other as possible. In this way immigration rates between the fragments will be increased, thereby maximizing the chances of extinct populations being replaced from elsewhere in the reserve complex (after [4])

71

extent of rare and massive disturbances to the landscape. Some of these catastrophic events can affect large areas and could have serious consequences in small reserves. Clearly a reserve in the best of all possible worlds would be considerably larger than the largest likely disturbance patch. In practice this is unlikely to be achieved!

Given a large reserve it should not be dissected by open roads or power lines. Many species, particularly those living in tropical rainforest, are psychologically incapable of crossing such barriers and for them they effectively reduce the area of the reserve.

Several small reserves will be better than no reserve at all, but they will hold fewer species at equilibrium than will a single reserve of the same total area. The small reserves will be best placed close together, so that each may act as a source area for the others. In this way their equilibrial numbers of species will be raised due to increased immigration rates. This effect will be enhanced if the small reserves are connected by corridors or stepping stones of suitable habitat. These general rules are illustrated in Fig. 8.4.

Simberloff and Abele [9] have suggested that a series of small reserves may have some advantages over a single large reserve. They will be less susceptible to natural catastrophes such as a disease epidemic or huge forest fire. They may also allow the survival of a group of competitors, one of which would exclude the others from a single reserve. Finally a series of reserves may be better for preserving a range of rare and scattered habitats.

In practice, the area and location of a reserve will always be a compromise between competing political, economic and local interests. The design rules set out above are of course general guidelines only and are no substitute for detailed ecological study of the community to be preserved. However, backed by the empirical evidence of insular studies, conservationists should be in a stronger position than before when competing for the shrinking land surface of our world.

References

[1] Brown, J. H. (1971), *Am. Nat.*, **105**, 467–478.
[2] Case, T. J. (1975), *Ecology*, **56**, 3–18.
[3] Diamond, J. M. (1972), *Proc. Nat. Acad. Sci.*, **69**, 3199–3203.
[4] Diamond, J. M. (1975), *Biol. Conservation*, **7**, 129–146.
[5] Diamond, J. M. (1976), *Proc. 16th Int. Ornith. Congr.*, pp. 616–628, Aust. Acad. Sci., Canberra.
[6] Diamond, J. M. & May, R. M. (1976), *Theoretical Ecology* (ed. May, R. M.), pp. 163–187, Blackwell, Oxford.
[7] Moore, N. W. & Hooper, M. D. (1975), *Biol. Conservation*, **8**, 239–250.
[8] Pickett, S. T. A. & Thompson, J. N. (1978), *Biol. Conservation*, **13**, 27–38.
[9] Simberloff, D. S. & Abele, L. G. (1976), *Science*, **191**, 285–286.
[10] Sullivan, A. L. & Schaffer, M. L. (1975), *Science*, **189**, 13–17.
[11] Willis, E. O. (1974), *Ecol. Monogr.*, **44**, 153–169.
[12] Wilcox, B. A. (1978), *Science*, **199**, 996–998.

OVERLEAF

Map of the world showing location
of islands mentioned in the text

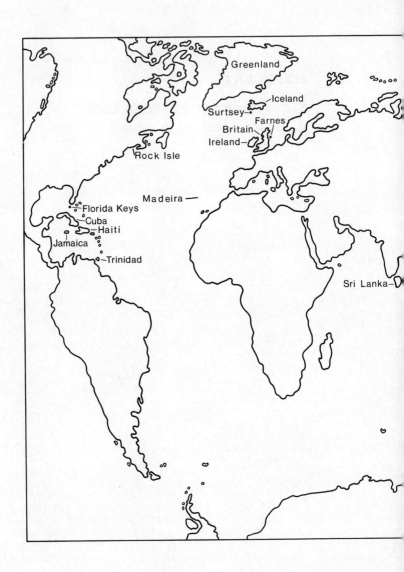

Vancouver Island—

California
Channel Islands—.

Hawaiian
oo—Islands

Gulf of
California Islands

—Formosa

Barro Colorado—

New Guinea
Borneo / Karkar
Long Island
New Ireland
New Britain
—Solomons

Puercos

Galapagos—

tau
a

New Hebrides
oo—Samoa

Fiji
.—Tonga

New Caledonia

ng Island—

—New Zealand

Tasmania

Furneaux
Group

Index